© Éditions de la Réunion des musées nationaux
Paris 2004
49, rue Étienne Marcel – 75001 Paris
ISBN 2-7118-4764-0
GG 20 4764

Musée d'Orsay
The Guide to the Collections

by Caroline **Mathieu**
Chief curator

M'O

Welcome to the Musée d'Orsay

The Musée d'Orsay is unique. It is the museum of the second half of the nineteenth century and the early twentieth century. It is the museum of *The Fife Player* and *Olympia*, the museum of Courbet and Monet, the home of Impressionism and Symbolism, the museum of *The Angelus* and the *Bal du Moulin de la Galette*; the place to find Carpeaux and Rodin, Puvis de Chavannes' *Poor Fisherman* and Degas' pastels; it is the museum of Guimard and Gallé, and that of photography, with Charles Nègre and Eugène Atget. It is housed in an old railway station designed by Victor Laloux in 1900. It has attracted nearly 50 million visitors since it opened in 1986 and is still a major draw today. Admittedly, it has much to offer.

It is located in central Paris, in the Saint Germain district on the left bank of the Seine. Across the river are the Tuileries gardens with the Louvre on the right and the Grand Palais looming up beyond the bridges further off.

The stone building has a gracious façade overlooking the Seine. The long central part has a rhythmic design with seven great arches, surmounted by a decorative band of cartouches and garlands and three huge allegorical statues. It is flanked by two jutting pavilions, each with a large clock set in a semi-circular cornice which make the original function of the building quite clear.

The main entrance has been moved to the side, on the western façade, which was once a de luxe hotel. The hotel stayed in operation longer than the station itself and its dining and reception rooms have been preserved and restored. The iron and glass canopy now shelters the entrance to the museum. The terrace in front of it is dotted with statues of animals and allegories of the continents, which were shown at the Universal Exhibition of 1878; the subject matter, spectacular size and position of the statues have a startling impact, intriguing visitors and adding a lively touch to the forecourt.

Once inside, visitors are struck by the originality of the building and the way it has been used as they gaze along the monumental nave of the former railway station, with its semi-circular vault, caisson ceiling, glass roofs for overhead lighting, and the glass and iron curtain walls that close off the tympanums. The great nave has been preserved in all its majesty, like the nave of a basilica and its golden light creates a magical atmosphere.

The next thrill comes from the art works themselves: first the statues set out on a series of stepped landings stretching to the far end of the nave and higher up on the terraces of the pavilions on either side. The sculpture from this period was much decried in the twentieth century but has gradually been rehabilitated through its presentation in the Musée d'Orsay, where great care has been taken to show it to advantage. The finest work by sculptors from Pradier to Carpeaux – Clésinger, Préault, Dubois, Mercié, Cordier, Falguière, Barrias, Dalou and Fremiet – now stands alongside sculptures by artists such as Daumier, Degas and Gauguin, while the works of Bartholomé, Rodin, Bourdelle, Meunier, Maillol, Rosso, Joseph Bernard and Pompon express other visions and lead sculpture in new directions.

The Musée d'Orsay's greatest asset is its multidisciplinary approach: it encompasses sculpture, painting and pastels, drawings, the decorative arts, a section on architecture and a collection of photographs which is an integral part of the whole and was a real innovation in the French museum world when it was first created.

The painting collection is scattered throughout the museum. The section on the second half of the nineteenth century, a crucial period in art history because of its fertility and brilliance, is the biggest and finest collection in the world. Paintings by

Courbet, Millet, Corot and the Barbizon school are introduced by works by Delacroix, Ingres, Chassériau and Daumier, which make a neat transition with the Louvre. Puvis de Chavannes comes next with easel paintings unlike anything produced at the time: *Girls By the Sea* or *The Dream* reveal a new idea of painting deeply rooted in tradition and yet utterly new. Then the art of the grand masters of Impressionism is represented by full sets of works by Manet, Monet, Renoir, Bazille, Caillebotte, Pissarro, Sisley, Degas and Cézanne, which illustrate the development of each artist and various aspects of their thinking. People come from all over the world to see *Lunch on the Grass* by Manet, *Poppies, near Argenteuil* by Monet, *The Swing* by Renoir, *The Star* by Degas, *The Hanged Man's House* by Cézanne. These works have become universal and are often the centre of attention.

Tastes change and art history changes with them: the other styles from this period, which were long dismissed as conventional and academic and condemned to oblivion, are gradually regaining their place. The distinction between the artists regarded as "good" and "bad" at the time has gradually blurred because it does not reflect the complexity of historical reality or the obvious criteria of artistic quality. One of the strengths of the Musée d'Orsay is its ability to display the diversity of other trends, setting idealised painting alongside works that swear by realism, with artists such as Cabanel, Gérôme, Delaunay, Meissonier, Ribot, Bonnat, Tissot, Carolus-Duran, Gervex, Stevens, Jules Breton, Bastien-Lepage, Laurens, Cormon, Detaille, De Neuville, and adding some of the greatest masterpieces by artists who defy classification such as Fantin-Latour, Whistler and Carrière.

Pierre Puvis de Chavannes
1824-1898
The Dream. "In his sleep, he sees love, glory and riches appear before him"
1883
Oil on canvas
82 x 102 cm

The Impressionist movement, which challenged everything and fashioned the future, was followed by Cézanne and his accomplished *Portrait of Gustave Geffroy*, brimming with possibilities, Seurat and *The Circus*, Van Gogh and *The Church at Auvers*, Gauguin and *The White Horse* and the Pont Aven school. Symbolism, announced by Gustave Moreau and guided by Puvis de Chavannes, found a leader in Odilon Redon, who is magnificently represented by a set of paintings, pastels and drawings and decorative panels from Domecy. Toulouse-Lautrec has a whole room to himself. The Nabis, Sérusier, Denis, Bonnard, Vuillard, Roussel and Vallotton, represent the last great movement in French painting around 1900 to be housed in the Musée d'Orsay; the Fauves, who came later and are in the Centre Georges Pompidou, are evoked here by a few masterpieces by Matisse, Vlaminck and Derain, which show the influence of Divisionism and the spirit of continuity. Away from the mainstream movements, Douanier Rousseau's highly individual genius shows through in two of his greatest works: *War* and *The Snake Charmer*, while the "foreign schools" as they used to be called, are represented by a number of outstanding works by Vilhelm Hammershøi, Georg Hendrik Breitner and Gustav Klimt. The Musée d'Orsay thus offers a panorama of painting from 1848 to 1914 in all its variety and profusion, revealing its crazes and unfairness, its passions and its blindness, its conformism and daring. It is so inventive, accomplished and innovative that it still speaks to us today and is an enduring source of values for our time.

Sculpture, already mentioned because it is so closely linked to the layout of the museum, provides a similar panorama in its subject matter, materials, techniques and forms. Its great diversity expresses everything from convention to convulsion, from affectation to grandeur, from the commonplace to the universal. Architecture, which is so difficult to present well in a museum, is mainly represented by a remarkable set of 18,000 drawings. They are displayed on a rotational basis in the new prints and drawings gallery, alternately with a selection of drawings featuring exhaustive sets or rare pieces by the greatest masters, Millet, Puvis de Chavannes, Degas and Seurat, or lesser known artists such as Bénouville, Harpignies and Ménard. The decorative arts take up a whole section of the museum because the period was so rich in this field and the objects, furniture and jewellery in the collection are highly representative. The exuberance and eclecticism of pieces designed during the Second Empire and the Third Republic (*Medal Cabinet* by Diehl and Fremiet) is balanced by the restraint and idealism of the *Arts and Crafts* movement (Morris, Dresser, Godwin) and the Glasgow school (Mackintosh), the Art Nouveau movement in France (Gallé, Guimard, Daum, Marjorelle, Charpentier), Belgium (Van de Velde, Horta, Hankar) and Catalonia (Gaudi), the Viennese Sezession (Hoffmann, Moser, Wagner, Loos) and the German *Werkbund* (Behrens), which revolutionised interior design and individual lifestyles and laid the foundations for twentieth century design. The photographic collection is not the least important part of the complex, living organism known as the Musée d'Orsay. It was set up from scratch and now contains 50,000 prints, telling the history of photography from its invention by Nicéphore Niepce in 1839 through to the early 1920s and illustrating the work of its main practitioners Le Gray, Bayard, Nègre, Nadar, technical progress, the main genres, portraits, landscapes, composition, photo assignments, documentary and scientific photos and the various movements from the Heliographic Mission to Pictorialism down to Eugène Atget and Alfred Stieglitz.

All these works are part of the collections of the French Republic. They have been purchased, donated or bequeathed and make up an artistic heritage of the highest value, famous throughout the world, very much in demand and admired by visitors from all continents. It was for them that this guide was designed and written by Caroline Mathieu, head curator of the Musée d'Orsay, with her perfect knowledge of the subject, great sense of discernment, and her sensitive analysis written in a clear, succinct style. The guide alone makes it easy to see why the Musée d'Orsay is truly unique.

Serge **Lemoine**
Chairman of the public
corporation of the musée d'Orsay

CONTENTS

The History of the Station and the Museum

The Orsay railway station grew out of the need felt by all major railway companies to have a terminus close to the city centre. The Compagnie des Chemins de Fer d'Orléans considered that the Austerlitz station's outlying location was a particular drawback and in 1897, shortly before the 1900 Universal Exhibition, it persuaded the state to part with a centrally located property on the Quai d'Orsay. The ruins of the Palais d'Orsay – the Audit Office – which had been destroyed by fire during the Commune in 1871 were still standing on the site.

The station project aroused fears that one of the most beautiful sites in Paris would be disfigured by a grimy, noisy, industrial building. To pacify the critics, the company asked three well-known architects, Emile Bénard, Lucien Magne and Victor Laloux, to submit projects for the museum. Laloux's project was selected in 1898. Laloux had won the Grand Prix de Rome in 1878 and taught architecture at the Ecole des Beaux-Arts; he had designed many buildings for his home town of Tours (Saint Martin Basilica, City Hall, the railway station) and later, in 1908, he participated in the construction of the Crédit Lyonnais building. He designed a monumental station, with stone facades, and a 370-room hotel opening on to the rue de Bellechasse and the rue de Lille.

Laloux planned the entire decoration down to the tiniest details, in a lavish eclectic style, and was probably instrumental in selecting the artists who executed the work, most of whom were official painters and sculptors. The departure hall was decorated by Ferdinand Cormon, the restaurant by Gabriel Ferrier (*Allegory of Time*) and Benjamin Constant *(Sky Roads),* and the reception room by Pierre Fritel *(Apollo's Chariot).* The facade facing the Seine is punctuated by three great sculptures, symbolising the cities of Toulouse by Laurent Marqueste, Bordeaux by

The Orsay railway station
by the architect Victor
Laloux, 1850-1937

The great clock in the
central aisle

Jean-Baptiste Hugues, and Nantes by Jean-Antoine Injalbert, whose statue has the features of the architect's wife. The station was brought into operation in May 1900 and officially opened on 14 July that year; it was the first modern railway station to be built for electric locomotives, which explains the luxurious nave and high vault decorated with painted stucco floral motifs, conjuring up the atmosphere of the great baths and basilicas of the Roman Empire. The design included luggage hoists and ramps, passenger lifts and fifteen tracks that ran under the quay and the Caisse des Dépôts. But the equipment quickly became obsolete. Mainline traffic ceased in 1939, although the hotel continued to operate until 1973. The building then became a great stone and glass wasteland, and a venue for various events and activities; it was used as a reception centre for homecoming prisoners in 1945, Orson Welles filmed *The Trial* there in 1962 and for a time it was the home of the Renaud-Barrault Theatre Company.

In 1973, in response to the wishes of the French Museums Authority, Georges Pompidou's government launched a project to convert the station into a museum to house late nineteenth- and early twentieth-century art, as a link between the Louvre and the National Museum of Modern Art (Centre Georges Pompidou). So the station, which had long been regarded as a monster of fin-de-siècle bad taste, was saved from demolition and replacement by a gigantic hotel, but only after a crime against architecture - the destruction of Baltard's marketpavilions at Les Halles, amid a general outcry, in 1972. The Orsay project was approved by Georges Pompidou and supported by later presidents, Valéry Giscard d'Estaing and François Mitterrand.

A planning study was commissioned in 1974 to assess the buildings and the feasibility of their use as a museum. In 1979, ACT Architecture (Renaud Bardon, Pierre Colboc and Jean-Pierre Philippon) won the state-run competition. Their project put the entrance to the museum in the rue de Bellechasse, hollowed out the great nave to house the collections, and constructed rooms on either side of

Ahead of Mercury,
patron of travellers,
crowns the station's two
metal gables

Alfred Jacquemart
1824-1896
Rhinoceros
1878
Cast iron
286 x 229 x 378 cm

Pierre Rouillard
1820-1881
Plough horse
1878
Cast iron
350 x 223 x 220 cm

a centre aisle, topped with terraces which opened at each level under the domes of the old station. A long gallery with overhead lighting was installed under the roof. The hotel's reception rooms were included in the circuit and its dining room became the museum's restaurant. Laloux's metal pillars and beams and his stucco decoration were carefully restored and the presence of the original building is clearly perceptible within the new structures. The next step was the layout of the rooms, and the choice of materials, colours and display equipment, which was left to the Italian architect Gae Aulenti in 1980. She chose a strong architectural design that could withstand the overwhelming volume of the station and Laloux's decoration and sought to unify the museum's galleries by lining all the walls and floors, except the Impressionist gallery, with Buxy stone, a flamed limestone from Burgundy. The colour scheme distinguished the original green metal framework from the new blue or brown structures.

Opened to the public on 9 December 1986, the Musée d'Orsay has already attracted nearly 50 million visitors.

From left to right
Pierre-Alexandre Schœnewerk
1820-1885
Alexandre Falguière
1831-1900
Eugène Delaplanche
1836-1890
Ernest Eugène Hiolle
1834-1886
Mathurin Moreau
1822-1912
Aimé Millet
1819-1891

The Six Continents :
Europe, Asia, Africa,
North America, Oceania,
South America
1878
Cast iron

Painting

Jean-Auguste-Dominique Ingres and Eugène Delacroix, two powerful personalities who incarnate the conflict between the Classical and Romantic movements, dominated painting in France throughout the 1850s. Both artists were born in the late eighteenth century and they are represented in the Musée d'Orsay only by later works and by the paintings of artists whom they influenced directly or who borrowed aspects of their subject matter, style, form or colour. But most of the work of Ingres and Delacroix belongs to the first half of the nineteenth century and is displayed in the Louvre.

Ingres pushed to the extreme his taste for arabesques, curving lines and distortions, as can be seen in *Venus at Paphos* (1852-1853), in which the supple line of the goddess' back and the set of her neck and breast form a series of answering curves. The countryside was painted by one of Ingres' pupils and assistants, Alexandre Desgoffe. *The Spring,* begun in Florence in 1820 and completed in Paris in 1856, harmoniously unfolds the flowing curve of her body, highlighted by the thrusting hip so characteristic of Ingres' nudes.

Ingres' influence on pupils in his own studio is particularly apparent in the work of Amaury Duval and Hippolyte Flandrin. Amaury Duval was a talented portraitist, with an elegant style and a strange use of colour (*Madame de Loynes,* 1862), while Flandrin's portraits (*Prince Napoleon*, 1860) show sobriety, rigour and balance.

It is worth noting, too, the emergence of the Neo-Greek group, attracted by Antiquity and Ingres' art, and represented by Jean-Léon Gérôme. Gérôme's painting *The Cock Fight* (1846) reveals a taste for a fine finish, clear colours and smooth paintwork. He also sought to give new impetus to religious painting: the astonishing staging of *Jerusalem (Golgotha, Consummatum est,* 1867) restored the deep mystery and power of suggestion of the Gospel story.

Ingres was a genius of form, line and drawing and, although he remained a solitary figure, many great painters, such as Gustave Moreau, Puvis de Chavannes and Degas, have acknowledged their debt to him.

Jean-Auguste-Dominique Ingres
1780-1867
The Spring
1820-1856
Oil on canvas
163 x 80 cm
Bequest of the Comtesse
Duchâtel, 1878

Romanticism under the Second Empire
Eugène Delacroix, Théodore Chassériau

"Never have more beautiful, more intense colours flowed through the eye to the soul," Baudelaire noted in his *Salon de 1855*. This comment on Delacroix's *The Lion Hunt*, in the Bordeaux Museum, the upper part of which was destroyed during the 1870 fire, applies just as well to the large sketch in the Musée d'Orsay which is a slight variant of the Bordeaux composition. Its spirited tone, swift, violent brushstrokes, range of yellows, orange, brown and red set off by a few touches of blue and green make *The Lion Hunt* a powerful, innovative painting. The same free brushwork and emphasis on colour are found in two other famous paintings by Delacroix (*Arab Horses Fighting in a Stable*, 1860; *Fording a Stream in Morocco*, 1858). Paul Huet, a close friend of Delacroix, perpetuated his Romantic approach to landscape until late in the century, with brio, as demonstrated by *The Chasm*, 1861.

Theodore Chassériau, Ingres' pupil and an admirer of Delacroix, created an original oeuvre by reconciling "two rival schools of drawing and colour". *The Tepidarium* (1853) inspired by one of the baths discovered at Pompeii, combines a taste for line with a feeling for colour, and exalts the oriental languor of Ingres as well as that of Delacroix.

Théodore Chassériau
1819-1856
The Tepidarium
1853
Oil on canvas
171 x 258 cm
Purchased in 1853

Eugène Delacroix
1798-1863
The Lion Hunt
Study of 1854
Oil on canvas
86 x 115 cm
Purchased in 1984

The Grand Prix de Rome was always a guarantee of a brilliant career in the arts. As the culmination of years of training at the Ecole des Beaux-Arts, the prize included a sojourn in the Villa Médicis in Rome and was usually followed by admission to the Académie des Beaux-Arts and appointment to a teaching position at the Ecole des Beaux-Arts. Everything was laid before these artists – official commissions, ceremonial portraits, and an opportunity to exhibit at the Salons – and their work was accomplished and idealised. Alexandre Cabanel, William Bouguereau, Robert Delaunay, Paul Baudry and Jean-Jacques Henner all trod the official path.

Alexandre Cabanel achieved fame with his history paintings with their studied composition, precise execution and accurate details (*Death of Francesca de Rimini and Paolo Malatesta*, 1870) and was even better known for his idealised mythological nudes. Thus *The Birth of Venus* (1863), exhibited at the 1863 Salon, was extremely popular and was bought by Napoleon III, while Manet's *Déjeuner sur l'herbe*, considered obscene, was rejected. The jutting hip and sinuous line of Venus's body reveal the influence of Ingres. However, Zola described her as follows: "The goddess, drowning in a stream of milk, looks like a delectable lorette, not modelled in flesh and bone – that would be indecent – but in a sort of pink and white almond paste." Cabanel was a talented portraitist, too, rendering the character of *Countess Keller* (1873) with an acid touch.

The Second Empire appreciated the talent of society portraitists, such as the German painter Franz Xaver Winterhalter who was the official court portraitist. *Madame Rimsky-Korsakov* (1864) testifies to his virtuosity in capturing the sensuality of his model.

Paul Baudry took his inspiration from Titian in *Fortune and the Child*, exhibited in the 1857 Salon. His major work is the decoration of the grand foyer of the Paris Opera House, which he painted for his friend Charles Garnier, along with a vibrant portrait of the architect. The Italian Renaissance also inspired Jean-Jacques Henner in *Chaste Suzanne*, 1864, whose sturdy flesh is rendered in a rich layer of paint.

"Crueller than war, vice has taken hold of Rome and is avenging the conquered world" (Juvenal, 6th satire). Thomas Couture painted in an ambitious style with great brio and virtuosity; he initiated a trend towards eclecticism and his studio attracted a great crowd, including Manet. *The Romans of the Decadence*, exhibited at the 1847 Salon, referred particularly to Veronese and Tiepolo.

Weary of the omnipresence of Italian influences, Henri Regnault, a talented painter who met an early death fighting in the 1870 war, took his cue from Velasquez and Goya and indulged in Romantic fervour (*General Prim*, 1869) or sumptuous displays of oriental cruelty (*Execution without Trial of the Moorish Kings of Grenada*, 1870).

Alexandre Cabanel
1823-1889
The Birth of Venus
1863
Oil on canvas
130 x 225 cm

Purchased for Napoleon
III in 1863 and assigned
to the Musées nationaux
in 1879

Franz Xaver Winterhalter
1806-1873
Madame Rimsky-Korsakov
1864
Oil on canvas
117 x 90 cm
Gift of Madame Rimsky-
Korsakov and her sons,
1879

Henri Regnault
1843-1871
*Execution without Trial
of the Moorish Kings
of Grenada*
1870
Oil on canvas
306 x 146 cm
Purchased in 1872

Thomas Couture
1815-1879
The Romans of the
Decadence
1847
Oil on canvas
466 x 775 cm
Commissioned in 1846

Honoré Daumier

Forming a link between Romanticism and Realism, a multifaceted genius who was not only a great painter, a keenly expressive sculptor but also a draughtsman and a lithographer, Honoré Daumier has a special place among his generation.

Daumier began his career as a painter in his forties when he entered the competition organised by the short-lived Second Republic in 1848. *The Republic Feeding and Instructing her Children* was chosen from the five hundred entries in a contest organised by the temporary Republican government, which wanted to celebrate its victory and the fall of Louis-Philippe. But the project was not followed through and no winner was chosen. The painting is striking for its monumentality and expressive power, its warm tones of rust and brown, a slightly translucent green, and its decisive, generous brushstrokes. The composition was inspired by allegories of Charity, through the iconographic legacy of Antiquity and the Renaissance.

Daumier showed the same baroque power in his painting as in his sculpture. *The Thieves and the Donkey* (1858) is a convulsive tangle of shapes with a wild, colourful rhythm. Stage lighting gave him an opportunity to use violently contrasted light effects which accentuate facial features and distortions and help build character (*Crispin and Scapin*, circa 1864). The subject matter and his treatment of it were completely new and the lesson was not lost on many artists of the time, such as Degas and Toulouse-Lautrec.

Honoré Daumier
1808-1879
Crispin and Scapin
circa 1864
Oil on canvas
60.5 x 82 cm
Gift of the Société des amis du Louvre, with help from the children of Henri Rouart, 1912

Honoré Daumier
1808-1879
The Laundress
circa 1863
Oil on wood
49 x 33.5 cm
Purchased with help from
D. David Weill, 1927

Alfred Chauchard (1822-1909) was one of the founders of the Grands Magasins du Louvre. From 1885 onwards, he built an art collection with a preference for nineteenth-century French painting, especially Jean-François Millet and the landscape painters of the Barbizon group (Théodore Rousseau, Jules Dupré, Narcisse Diaz de la Peña, Camille Corot, Charles-François Daubigny...). Chauchard left his collection to the Louvre in 1909.

The important place given to peasant figures in the art of the period corresponds to the rural exodus and the nostalgia that accompanied it as a large part of the population flowed towards cities in the throes of industrial expansion. It is significant that Alfred Chauchard's first major purchase, in 1890, was Millet's *The Angelus* (1858-1859), which he wrested from American collectors. Millet's paintings showed peasants in their natural setting; thus *The Angelus* shows two static figures, monumental in their simplicity, drawn in a vigorous, synthetic manner, who seem to be planted in the depths of the earth which rises towards the horizon like a sea. The brushstrokes are dense and the tones are muted. It is a powerful image and its extraordinary popularity has done it a disservice. Reproduced on all manner of objects, copied and caricatured, *The Angelus* was soon familiar even in the remotest rural districts.

Born at Gruchy near Cherbourg, Millet started his career as a portraitist for the middle class in Normandy. His early works were strongly structured and richly coloured (*Madame Lecourtois*, circa 1841; *Madame Canoville*, 1845); the Thomas Henry Museum, Cherbourg, has a magnificent set of these portraits. *The Bathers*, 1848, is a youthful work which demonstrates Millet's masterly rendering of the human body, which is strongly outlined, and gives weight and density to the peasants in his painting. This is shown in *The Gleaners*, 1857, whose deliberate sculptural heaviness is rendered by means of simplified form; these figures, who could

Narcisse Diaz de la Peña
1807-1876
The Heights of Jean de Paris
1867
Oil on canvas
84 x 106 cm
Alfred Chauchard bequest, 1909

Théodore Rousseau
1812-1867
*An Avenue, Forest
of Isle-Adam*
1849

Oil on canvas
101 x 82 cm
Alfred Chauchard bequest,
1909

Jean–François Millet
1814-1875
The Angelus
1858-1859
Oil on canvas
55 x 66 cm
Alfred Chauchard bequest,
1909

Jean-François Millet
1814-1875
The Gleaners
1857
Oil on canvas
83.5 x 111 cm

Gift from Mrs Pommery
(with life interest), 1890;
entered in 1890

Jean-François Millet
1814-1875
Spring
1868-1873
Oil on canvas
86 x 111 cm
Gift from Mrs Frédéric
Hartman, 1887

have stepped out of a low relief, are doing their work in a ritual manner, slowly and nobly. Their heavy, threadbare clothing is rendered in muted tones but the pinks and blues are still vivid.

Since 1849, Millet had been part of the group of painters at Barbizon, a village on the fringe of the Fontainebleau forest. The group introduced landscape painting as a major theme, as well as the habit of painting direct from nature; what had previously been merely the backdrop became the main subject for this group of artists attracted by forests, ponds, undergrowth, trees and clearings. These motifs are particularly well illustrated by Théodore Rousseau, the most important figure in the group. Fascinated by the elusive effects of light, Rousseau captured the weightiness of the midday sun in summer (*An Avenue, Forest of Isle-Adam,* 1849*),* and the "dark light" of the storm (*The Pond, Stormy Sky,* circa 1860-1865). *The Resting Place at Bas Bréau,* which he began in winter 1836-1837, was reworked throughout the painter's life. Jules Dupré worked in a sombre Romantic mood, while Narcisse Diaz de la Peña, who made friends with Rousseau in 1837, attempted to catch the dappled effect of light in foliage (*The Heights of Jean de Paris,* 1862).

After 1860, Millet concentrated increasingly on landscapes, painting the villages and hills of his native Cotentin. *The Church at Gréville* (1871-1874), with its impressive perspective and soulful atmosphere, spoke directly to painters like Van Gogh. At the end of his life, Millet painted landscapes charged with violent lyricism; *Spring,* part of the unfinished *Four Seasons* series (1868-1873), reveals the influence of Salomon van Ruysdael and John Constable in its range of tender greens, the rainbow and the taste for nature's sudden sombre displays. At the same time, Millet produced large pastels that illustrate his exceptional talent as a draughtsman.

Charles-François Daubigny, attracted by outdoor painting, often stayed at Barbizon after 1843; he sailed on the Seine and the Oise in his floating studio, *Le Botin,* and was one of the first to try to catch fleeting effects, the mobility of the instant, with rapid brushwork and pale colours (*Château Gaillard,* 1877). *The Harvest* (1851) with its broad horizon and pale sky of juxtaposed pure colour is an early promise of the Impressionists' instantaneous view of nature. *Snow,* painted in winter 1842-1873, impressive in its emptiness and vigorous manner, its contrasting blacks and whites and low reddening sky reveals his contacts with the Impressionists.

Camille Corot, born in the eighteenth century, developed his second period of lyrical, misty painting in the 1850s. He was working on the outskirts of Paris and was influenced by the soft, pearly grey, diffused light of the Ile de France region. His landscapes were peopled with nymphs: *Dancing Nymphs* (circa 1860-1865). Corot also favoured isolated figures, often in fanciful costumes, with a melancholic or mysterious air (*Corot's Studio, Young Woman with a Mandolin,* circa 1865-1870; *Seated Man in Armour,* circa 1868-1870).

As they are linked to the Romantic Movement and the first half of the nineteenth century, works by the Barbizon school and Corot have stayed in the Louvre.

Charles-François Daubigny
1817-1878
Snow
1873
Oil on canvas
90 x 120 cm
Accepted in lieu
of inheritance tax, 1989

**Jean-Baptiste-Camille
Corot**
1796-1875
Nymphs Dancing
Circa 1860-1865
Oil on canvas
98 x 131 cm
Purchased in 1851

"How could anyone paint such ghastly people?" "It would put you off being buried at Ornans." So the critics greeted the scandal of the 1850 Salon, *A Burial at Ornans* (1849-1850), a manifesto of the detested Realism in the name of which they vilified the works of Courbet and Millet. The realism here lies in the truthfulness of what is shown – the place, the identifiable people presented just as they were and, for many of them, that meant ugly and common. There was novelty, too, in the large size of the picture, which raised a familiar episode to the rank of a history painting; the theme of death, funerals and cemeteries was already a favourite with the Romantics. A monumental, sculptural painting whose stolid weeping women have something of the weeping figures on the great Burgundian tombs of the late Middle Ages, *A Burial at Ornans* emphasises austerity and silence and reveals the beauty of Courbet's colours: a range of blacks each different from the last, heightened with touches of white, the strong accents of the red robes and duck-blue stockings. Delacroix, although he deplored the vulgarity of the figures, admitted that "there are superb details: the priests, the choirboys, the vase of holy water, and the weeping women."

Courbet painted *The Artist's Studio* for the 1855 Universal Exhibition; he used real figures to symbolise his loves and hates, the ideals he upheld and those he rejected, revealing his personal feelings and his artistic tastes. The painting was rejected by the jury of the Salon, along with *A Funeral* that Courbet wanted to exhibit with it, and so he arranged an exhibition of about forty of his works in a specially built booth that he called "The Pavilion of Realism". *The Artist's Studio* (1855) highlights all Courbet's qualities: a portraitist and landscape painter, an animal and still life painter, and sensitivity in the rendering of the female body (genres that he illustrated throughout his life). But what is peculiar to Courbet's paintings and particularly noticeable in *The Artist's Studio* is the mysterious, poetic mood, accentuated

Gustave Courbet
1819-1877
*The Artist's Studio,
a Real Allegory Describing
Seven Years of my Life
as an Artist and a Man*
1855
Oil on canvas
359 x 598 cm
Purchased by public
subscription and the
Friends of the Louvre,
1920

Gustave Courbet
1819-1877
The Spring
1868
Oil on canvas
128 x 97 cm
Purchased in 1919

Gustave Courbet
1819-1877
A Burial at Ornans
1849-1850
Oil on canvas
315 x 668 cm

Gift from Miss Juliette
Courbet, the artist's sister,
1881

by lighting from an indefinable source. Sometimes lit by a diffuse glow, sometimes artificially dim, *The Artist's Studio* gives the feeling of a dream world.

Alongside these great paintings, Courbet attracted a following for his portraits and landscapes; the success of paintings such as *Deer Taking Cover near the Stream at Plaisir Fontaine* (1866) or *Stag Fight* (1861) prompted him to return to such subjects frequently. *The Cliffs at Etretat After the Storm* (1869), a landscape with no human or anecdotal elements, with its clear, limpid atmosphere, makes it easy to understand the Impressionists' admiration for Courbet's light and frankness. Courbet settled in Etretat in 1869 and painted a tormented, disturbing *Stormy Sea* there. Guy de Maupassant tells of visiting Courbet: "In a big, bare room, a dirty, greasy, fat man was plastering white paint on a large, bare canvas with a kitchen knife. From time to time he went to lean his face against the window and stare at the storm. The sea was so close that it seemed to be beating against the house, which was engulfed in foam and noise. The saltwater struck the panes like hail and streamed down the walls. A bottle of cider stood on the mantelpiece beside a half empty glass. From time to time, Courbet went to take a sip and then came back to his work. That work became 'The Wave' and made quite a stir."

The Spring (1866), with its luminous, lifelike flesh, not only has the realism of experience, it carries us into the worlds of imagination and legend. Commissioned by the Turkish-Egyptian diplomat Khalil Bey, a picturesque figure in Paris during the Second Empire, *The Origin of the World* (1866) has a special place in Courbet's oeuvre. Although the female nude was one of the artist's favourite themes, he had never treated it in such an uninhibited way. It is a pure piece of painting, a straightforward representation of a woman's sex organs, rendered with freshness and lyricism. Khalil Bey was a discerning collector and already owned *The Turkish Bath* by Ingres (1862, Paris, Musée du Louvre) and another superb female nude by Courbet, *Sleep* (1866, Paris, Musée des Beaux-Arts de la Ville de Paris).

Gustave Courbet
1819-1877
*The Cliff at Etretat
after the Storm*
1869
Oil on canvas
133 x 162 cm
Painting Entrusted to
the National Museums
after the Second World
War

Gustave Courbet
1819-1877
Deer Taking Cover near the Stream at Plaisir Fontaine
1866

Oil on canvas
174 x 209 cm
Purchased by a group of art lovers who gifted it to the museum in 1890

Gustave Courbet
1819-1877
The Origin of the World
1866
Oil on canvas
46 x 55 cm
Accepted in lieu of inheritance tax, 1995

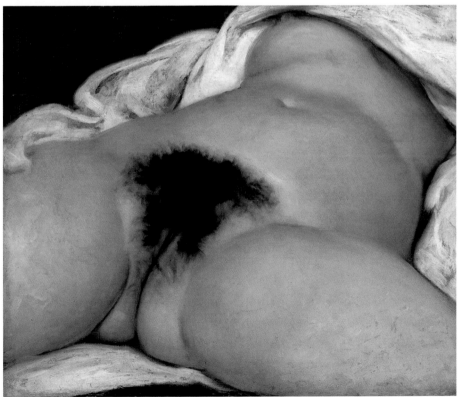

As assiduous observers of everyday life, regional customs and the changes and difficulties wrought by the relentless march towards an industrial society, painters such as Alexandre Antigna, Octave Tassaert, Isidore Pils and Jules Breton, alongside Daumier, Millet and Gustave Courbet, show the emergence of a realistic approach to painting. Some – Antigna, Pils and Breton – painted large canvases on contemporary, popular themes, with life-sized figures, hoping to see this frank, modern art raised to the rank of history painting.

Painted in the early stages of Realism, Antigna's *Lightning* (1848), although its mood is still dramatically Romantic, with its characters terrified by Nature's flashes, provides evidence of a modern sense of observation and presents life-size figures in a popular genre scene. This sense of drama is also to be found Tassaert's work, for instance in the state-commissioned painting *An Unhappy Family* (1849). Apart from its melodramatic side, it reveals the bitter reality of poverty. Evariste Luminais uses a range of grey and browns and a calm, matter-of-fact tone to convey the hardship of his *Family of Fishermen* (1865).

Isidore Pils, with *The Death of a Sister of Charity* (1850), took Realism a step further and gained recognition for a new category – religious genre scenes. Critics and art enthusiasts appreciated the nobility and dignity of the work, and praised the talent of an artist able to convey the full range of emotion in a picture painted in subdued tones, in a mood reminiscent of Philippe de Champaigne.

Originally tempted by realistic subjects in the same vein as those favoured by Antigna, Jules Breton turned to landscapes after 1853, focusing particularly on work in the fields, a genre which brought him instant success. *Calling in the Gleaners* won him a first class medal at the 1859 Salon and was immediately included in the national collections; this is the most famous painting of the series that Breton dedicated to the work in the fields at harvest time. The gleaners have a noble stature and the writer and critic Maxime du Camp expressed his admiration for Breton's "beautiful rustic caryatids".

Constant Troyon, initially drawn to the Barbizon school, discovered a vocation for animal painting after a trip to the Netherlands in 1847; he was particularly impressed by the art of Paulus Potter. From then on, Troyon worked on painting farm animals, sometimes changing his approach. The great popularity of animal painting can be explained by the expertise and ambition of artists such as Rosa

Isidore Pils
1823-1875
*Death of a Sister
of Charity*
1850
Oil on canvas
241 x 305 cm
Purchased from the artist,
1851

Jules Breton
1827-1906
Calling in the Gleaners
1859
Oil on canvas
90 x 176 cm
Gift from the Emperor
Napoléon III, 1862

Rosa Bonheur
1822-1899
Ploughing near Nevers;
First Dressing
1849

Oil on canvas
134 x 260 cm
Commissioned from the
artist in 1848

Bonheur, one of the most famous. *Ploughing in Nevers; First Dressing*, commissioned by the state in 1848, is still regarded by the public as a masterpiece of Realism, and is systematically compared to the writing of George Sand. A painter and sculptress, director of the Imperial School of Art and a court protégée, Rosa Bonheur quickly attained international reputation. Ernest Hébert is in a class of his own; he won the Prix de Rome in 1839 and spent several sojourns in Italy, but soon abandoned history painting to focus on scenes from popular life. His first great success, *Malaria* (1852) entered into the realistic mood of the day by testifying to the distress of the peasants debilitated by the illness that haunted the Pontine Marshes.

Meissonier was a much-liked artist whose paintings created a sensation and fetched high prices. With great skill and care he rendered, in the taste of the seventeenth-century Dutch masters, the calm, delicate mood of *Art Lovers* (1860), or *Man Reading* (1867). He also accurately rendered the effects of bright light (*Antibes, A Horse Ride*, 1869) or the dramatic nature of an historical episode (*The French Campaign*, 1814).

François Bonvin was associated with the Realist movement without really participating in it; he quietly recorded scenes from everyday life (*Servant Girl Drawing Water*, 1861), in sombre colours influenced by the Dutch painters of the seventeenth century which he liked to copy in the Louvre. His still lifes of animals *(Still Life with a Duck, Still Life with a Hare*, 1863) or peaceful studio scenes (*Still Life with a Palette*, 1863) show a bolder use of colours and bring out the subtlety of a sure hand and measured lighting. At the opposite extreme, Antoine Vollon, one of the most famous still life painters in the second half of the nineteenth century, cruelly portrayed the agony of *Fish from the Sea* (1870) in a totally realistic vein.

Théodule Ribot was influenced by seventeenth-century Spanish painters, Ribera in particular, illustrating religious themes such as *St Sebastian* (1865), dramatising his subject with strong contrasts of light and shade, thick paint and a clever use of blacks. He showed talent for domestic scenes, being also influenced by the seventeenth-century Dutch masters (*The Sermon*, circa 1890).

The painter Alphonse Legros, a friend of Fantin-Latour and follower of Courbet, was attracted by Hispanic mystic realism; *Making Amends* (1867) confirms his interest in the art of Francisco de Zurbarán.

Aldophe Monticelli, an admirer of Delacroix, and a friend of Diaz whose virtuosity deeply impressed him, was trained in Marseilles and attempted to create an enchanted, mysterious world in layers of oily brushstrokes (*Don Quixote and Sancho Panza*, circa 1865). He took a realistic approach to portraiture (*Madame Tessier*, 1872) and to his brightly coloured still lifes (*Still Life with a White Jug*, circa 1878-1880). Monticelli had a complex personality and although he continued to use Romantic themes, his bold colours and his taste for thick layers of paint later spoke to Vincent Van Gogh.

Ernest Meissonier
1815-1891
The French Campaign,
1814
1864
Oil on wood
57.5 x 76.5 cm
Alfred Chauchard bequest,
1909

Adolphe Monticelli
1824-1886
Still Life with a White Jug
Circa 1878-1880
Oil on canvas
49 x 63 cm
Gift from Gustave Fayet,
1911

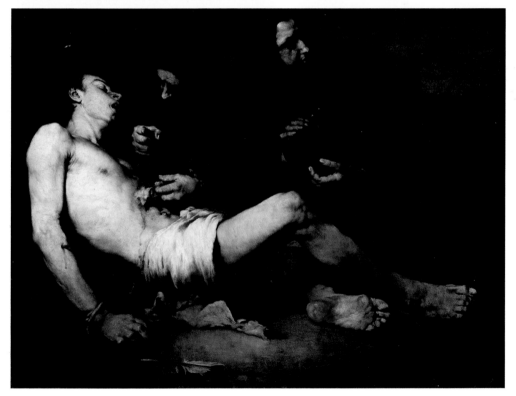

Théodule Ribot
1823-1891
The Martyrdom
of St Sebastian
1865
Oil on canvas
97 x 130 cm
Purchased from the artist
in 1865

The Orient has always fired the imagination, but it was particularly in the nineteenth century, thanks to Bonaparte and his Egyptian campaign, that the mysterious doors to these countries swung wide. After unreal visions of lascivious odalisques (Ingres) the Romantic generation threw itself passionately into the discovery of new landscapes and people, and brilliant, different colours. Then, whereas some, like Gérôme, presented a painstakingly realistic orientalism, nourished by souvenirs from their travels, others - Eugène Fromentin, and later Gustave Guillaumet and Léon Belly - were moved by the beauty of the countryside and its dazzling colours, and revealed the charm and the sometimes troubling nature of the Orient. Fromentin travelled in Algeria, published two memoirs and composed scenes nourished by his imagination and picturesque reconstitutions. But he was sometimes touched by the loneliness of the desert (*In the Land of Thirst,* 1867). Guillaumet, an inexperienced artist who used acrid colours, accumulated images of a grandeur that astounded and delighted his contemporaries (*Evening Prayer in the Sahara,* 1863). Fascinated by Algeria, where he stayed ten times or more, he captured the sincerity of picturesque scenes (*The Weavers at Bou Saada*). Guillaumet also conveyed the violence and fatality of a country of drought and blinding sunshine (*The Desert,* 1867). Belly, first attracted by the Barbizon landscape artists, set off for the Orient in 1840, visiting the Lebanon, Palestine and Egypt, where he later stayed on two occasions. In *Pilgrims on the Way to Mecca* (1861), the bold effect of the caravan moving towards the spectator was not universally appreciated, but the painting was a great success at the 1861 Salon and was counted as "one of the most remarkable paintings of our contemporary school and certainly the most truthful and striking yet inspired by the Orient." Charles Tournemine used vivid colours to render exotic subjects or imaginary visions inspired by travel accounts, such as *African Elephants* (1867).

Gustave Guillaumet
1840-1887
The Desert
1867
Oil on canvas
110 x 220 cm
Gift from the artist's
family, 1888

Charles de Tournemine
1812-1872
African Elephants
1867
Oil on canvas
88 x 178 cm
Purchased by Napoleon III
and gifted in 1867

"This man will be the painter, the true painter, who will make us see how grand and poetic we are in our ties and patent leather bootees," wrote Baudelaire, who hoped for a form of painting which would express the marvellous side of modernity; he found an echo in the work of Edouard Manet who was to bring out the contrasts, humour, poetry and beauty of his time.

Considered vulgar by the critics, the *Portrait of Monsieur and Madame Manet,* 1860, captured the image of a social type, that of the austere upper middle class of the Second Empire, as well as a striking psychological portrait of the artist's parents, which goes beyond the realism of their expressions. Although it owes a debt to Courbet, this portrait already announces some of the features proper to Manet's style: firm execution, a broad, bold stroke, and an original treatment of space in simplified planes. The first scandal broke with *Déjeuner sur l'herbe* (1863); the painting is part of Etienne Moreau-Nélaton's (1859-1927) outstanding collection. He was a painter himself, but also one of the great art historians of his time and a matchless patron. To the best paintings inherited from his grandfather, Adolphe Moreau (1800-1859), he added major works of the 1830s and built up the Impressionist section of the collection. In 1906, he gave the Louvre the finest donation of nineteenth-century paintings ever made to the national collections: 100 canvases including 37 Corots, 11 Delacroix, works by Alexandre-Gabriel Decamps, Théodore Géricault, Daumier (*The Republic),* Puvis de Chavannes (*The Dream*), Manet, Claude Monet, Berthe Morisot, Alfred Sisley and Camille Pissarro, Henri Fantin-Latour (*Homage to Delacroix,* 1864), as well as works by Maurice Denis, Paul-César Helleu, Albert Besnard, Aristide Maillol; a magnificent collection of drawings and watercolours (about 3,000 sheets and 100 sketchbooks) and numerous autographs (including 600 of Millet). Lastly, he left the French National Library a substantial collection of engravings and documents about the artists he had studied. The paintings of the Moreau-Nélaton collection are all in the Musée d'Orsay, while a suite of rooms in the Louvre is set aside for canvases from the "1830 school" (Corot, Delacroix, etc.).

Edouard Manet
1832-1883
Déjeuner sur l'herbe
(called *Bathing* in 1863)
1863

Oil on canvas
208 x 264.5 cm
Etienne Moreau-Nelaton
donation, 1906

Edouard Manet

Déjeuner sur l'herbe is undoubtedly the "historical" masterpiece of the collection. When Manet exhibited this painting at the 1863 Salon, he was already regarded by artists and some critics as the leader of a group experimenting with a new form of painting, while others reproached him precisely for his free, rapid technique, his "way of seeing in patches" and his modern subject matter. Despite its references to the old masters (Titian's *Fête Champêtre*, in the Louvre, and an engraving after Raphael), *Déjeuner sur l'herbe* was rejected by the jury, who proved so unfair that year that Napoleon III decided to open an alternative salon, famously known as the "Salon des Refusés". Painted in a clear light, with flowing rapid strokes, *Blonde Woman with Bare Breasts* (circa 1878) revealed the closer links between Manet and the Impressionists after the 1870 war. The scandal was even greater in 1865 when he presented *Olympia* (1863) at the Salon. This nude was judged "immoral" and ugly; indeed, Manet started from the ideal, a model inspired by Titian's *Venus of Urbino*, and moved towards the real, giving an individualised image. The lady is no Venus or odalisque, but a richly kept prostitute. This nude, crudely rendered by strong light and colour contrasts, is at the turning point between the Classical tradition and modern art. *Emile Zola* (1868) stoutly defended *Olympia* and Manet's painting, writing glowing articles in the press, and to thank him Manet painted his portrait in a setting that recalls his tastes and hobbies: Japanese prints, *Olympia,* and the brochure he had written on Manet.

Spanish painting was full of lessons for Manet, especially the work of Velasquez, of which we see traces in *The Fife Player* (rejected at the 1866 Salon) which shows a figure against a plain background, breaking the rules of traditional perspective. *The Balcony* (circa 1868-1869), presented at the 1869 Salon, takes up one of Goya's favourite themes. The figure in the foreground is Berthe Morisot, also an artist, who

Edouard Manet
1832-1883
Emile Zola
1868
Oil on canvas
146.3 x 114 cm
Gift from Madame Zola
(with a life interest), 1918;
Entered the museum
in 1925

Edouard Manet
1832-1883
*Blonde Woman with Bare
Breasts*
Circa 1878
Oil on canvas
62.5 x 52 cm
Etienne Moreau-Nelaton
donation, 1906

Edouard Manet
1832-1883
Olympia
1863
Oil on canvas
130.5 x 190 cm
Given to the state
by public subscription
on the initiative of
Claude Monet, 1890

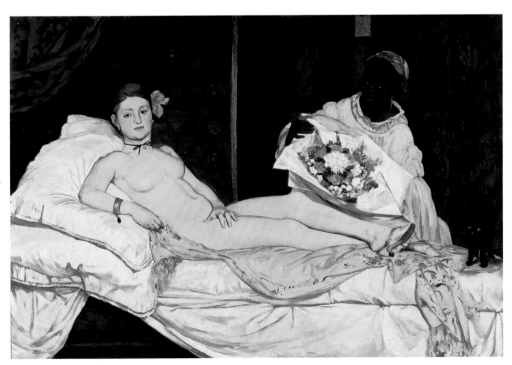

later married Manet's brother and showed her work in the Impressionists' exhibitions. As often in Manet's characters, she has a strangely fixed look, suggesting an inner dream out of reach of the spectator. This atmosphere, along with the aggressive green of the balcony against the delicate white muslin, disconcerted the critics. Manet often painted Berthe Morizot. In 1872, shortly after the Franco-Prussian War and the Commune which deeply affected him, he returned to painting. *Berthe Morisot with a Bunch of Violets* (1872) is sublimated by the magnificent use of black. The side-lit portrait, all light and shade, shows the young woman in an extravagant hat and brings out her charming blend of intelligence, passion and eccentricity. Incidentally, Pierre Puvis de Chavannes wrote to her: "Be nice and write to me everything that goes through your mind – through the mind that dwells in that strange, charming skull." This fascinating picture has always been admired, inspiring Paul Valéry, who talked of the "presence of absence" and found it poetic: "I can now say that the portrait I am talking about is pure *poetry*. By the strange harmony of the colours, by the dissonance of their forces; by the contrast between the trivial, ephemeral detail of an outmoded hairstyle and something elusively tragic in the facial expression, Manet has given his work resonance, creating mystery in the very firmness of his art. He has combined the physical likeness of the model, with the unique accord which suits a singular person, and has caught the distinct, abstract charm of Berthe Morisot."

After 1870, Manet drew closer to Monet and Renoir, working with them at Argenteuil, in the open air. His palette retained a new form of luminosity, as can be seen in *On the Beach*. Painted at Berck-sur-Mer in summer 1873, probably directly from nature, this picture clearly brings out Manet's original temperament, for on a theme often handled by Eugène Boudin or Monet, he has produced a work completely devoid of the picturesque. The distant, shady presence of an

Edouard Manet
1832-1883
*Berthe Morisot with
a Bunch of Violets*
1872
Oil on canvas
55 x 38 cm
Purchased with the aid
of the Heritage Fund,
the Meyer Foundation,
China Times Group and
private sponsorship
coordinated by the
newspaper *Nikkei*

Edouard Manet
1832-1883
The Balcony
Circa 1868-1869
Oil on canvas
170 x 124.5 cm
Gustave Caillebotte
bequest, 1894

ultramarine and emerald green sea is counterbalanced by the gravity of the two silhouettes in the foreground, painted in a classical harmony of grey and black. The painting has a Japanese tinge, with its very high horizon, underlined with dark blue, and its solid areas of colour. The sea attracted Manet once more in *Rochefort's Escape* (1880), but the entire space is devoted to the "marine plain", painted in a bright green with a lively brushstrokes. *Lady with Fans* (1873-1874) refers to an exotic, antique dealer's Japan, and shows Nina de Callias, a warm-hearted whimsical woman, who held one of the most highly appreciated literary and artistic salons of the time. Paul Verlaine and Charles-Marie Leconte de Lisle were among her regular visitors and Stéphane Mallarmé and Manet struck up a friendship there and saw one another almost daily for ten years. The portrait of *Stéphane Mallarmé* (1876) offers a familiar vision of the refined intellectual atmosphere, and the charm and elegance which united the two men. An unfailing friend of the Impressionists, *Georges Clemenceau* is forcefully portrayed by Manet whose quick, concise brushstrokes and sparing composition render the politician's energy, determination, and biting humour.

In the 1880s, Manet produced a growing number of small still lifes often as gifts for friends (*Asparagus*, 1880) or for the sheer joy of painting (*Lemon*, 1880; *Carnations and Clematis in a Crystal Vase*, circa 1882).

Edouard Manet
  1832-1883
  On the Beach
  1873
  Oil on canvas
  59.5 x 73.2 cm

Gift from J. Edouard
Dubrujeaud (with a life
interest), 1953;
entered the museum
in 1970

Henri Fantin-Latour
James Abbott McNeill Whistler

Although he was closely linked to the Impressionists, whom he admired and whose distaste for official painting he shared, Henri Fantin-Latour was in a category of his own. His first large painting, *Homage to Delacroix* (1864), is reminiscent of the collective portraits in seventeenth-century Holland, because of the grouping of the figures and its subdued rust, black and white tonality. Intended to pay Delacroix, who died in 1863, the homage he had not received in his lifetime, the painting shows the artist himself, Whistler with his mop of curly hair, a blond, luminous Manet, and Baudelaire's ravaged face. The critics saw nothing in his painting but a manifesto of Realist artists and a collection of likenesses; they expected heroism, an apotheosis, and found nothing but a reflection of contemporary life. The group was criticised for its lack of unity, harsh colour, and its static, photographic appearance.

Fantin-Latour's friendship with Manet and the future Impressionists shines through in *A Studio in Batignolles,* (1870), which is in fact a tribute to Manet, who is shown in his studio in the midst of his friends, the critic Zacharie Astruc, Renoir, Zola, the great Frédéric Bazille and Monet. The subject of the painting was accepted with little hostility and Fantin-Latour's talent was recognised by a medal at the Salon. This painting, like *A Corner of a Table* (1872), shows the artist's attempt to capture "correspondences", the spiritual links between people. *A Corner of a Table* is arranged in an original manner, ignoring traditional perspective, and centred on Verlaine and Arthur Rimbaud who stand deliberately apart from the group of honourable writers, who are now completely forgotten. The portraits of his friends and family (*Charlotte Dubourg,* 1882, his sister-in-law) also portray people shrouded in a sort of silent music, an inner greyness. His still lifes, like his portraits, reveal careful observation of reality: flowers, fruit and objects are surrounded by a pale, subtle light (*Flowers and Fruit,* 1865). At the other end of the scale, Fantin-Latour indulged in poetic compositions, creating a gentle, unreal world (*Night,* 1897) which was inspired by his passion for the music of Schumann, Wagner and Berlioz and gave rise to major series of lithographs.

James MacNeill Whistler was a good friend of Fantin-Latour's and closely connected to the Realist movement gathered around Courbet; he was an American who divided his time between London and France, but was only reluctantly accepted

Henri Fantin–Latour
1836-1904
A Studio in Batignolles
1870
Oil on canvas
204 x 273.5 cm
Purchased in 1892

Otto Scholderer
painter

Renoir

Zola

Edmond Maître
art lover

Bazille

Manet

Zacharie Astruc
writer, painter and
sculptor

Monet

Henri Fantin-Latour
James Abbott McNeill Whistler

in official circles in either country. His taste for Japanese art led him to simplify lines and seek refined harmonies of neutral tones, in his famous views of the Thames and in his portraits. *Arrangement in Grey and Black No 1* or *The Mother of the Artist* (1871), which joined the national collections under pressure from the poet Mallarmé and the critic Théodore Duret, is one of his most famous and universally admired works. Whistler used sparing lines, simple forms and a narrow colour range; he wrote about this painting: "To me it is interesting as a picture of my mother; but what can or ought the public to care about the identity of the portrait? ... A picture should have its own merit." On a steam boat ride on the Thames, Whistler was fascinated by the effect of the sunset and painted this fleeting vision in fluid, light strokes, strongly influenced by Japanese art (*Variations in Violet and Green,* 1871).

On the fringes of this group of artists interested in realism and new ideas, there developed a more official, bourgeois stream of realism, represented by Alfred Stevens, James Tissot and Carolus-Duran. Stevens was born in Brussels and painted scenes of Paris life during the Second Empire, a role he shared with James Tissot, who painted portraits of elegant, worldly society people (*Young Woman in a Red Jacket,* 1865). Courbet's influence could be felt in *The Convalescent* (1860) by Carolus-Duran, whereas *Lady with a Glove* (1869), shows his admiration for the colours and style of Velasquez and Van Dyck; this painting was so popular that the artist was swamped with commissions and fell prey to facility.

James Abbott McNeill Whistler
  1834-1903
  Arrangement in Grey and Black No. 1 or *The Mother of the Artist*

1871
Oil on canvas
144.3 x 162.5 cm
Purchased in 1891

In the 1850s and 1860s, two painters, Eugène Boudin and Johan-Barthold Jongkind, made direct observation their priority, taking their cue from the English artists (Constable, Richard Bonington, Joseph Mallord William Turner), as well as Corot and the Barbizon group who had already insisted on the need to capture fleeting atmospheric effects by working directly from nature.

It was the coast of Normandy, with its restless, cloudy skies, and constantly changing light that attracted these painters, often known as "Pre-Impressionists". Boudin, who was born in Honfleur, was fascinated by the sky and clouds; he met Monet, then Baudelaire and Courbet in 1859. Courbet encouraged him to paint seascapes: "You are the only one who really knows the sky," he said. *Camaret Port* (1872) or *Sailing Boats* (1869) gave the central place to the "beautiful sweeping skies, turbulent with clouds, streaked with colour, profound and rousing" that Boudin spoke of with such fondness. About 1862, he began to focus on the beaches of Deauville and Trouville made fashionable by an elegant, gay crowd (*Trouville Beach*, 1865; *Bathers on Trouville Beach*, 1869); this subject left him free to use pale colours and he tried to catch vibrancy of the light. Despite his travels (*Port of Bordeaux*, 1874; *Venice, Slave Quay*, 1895), Boudin remained profoundly attached to the Normandy coast.

Stanislas Lépine, a native of Caen, worked alone, away from the major movements of his time. He used delicate grey tones to catch the light and mood of his region in small paintings that banished all human forms (*Port of Caen*, 1859; *The Apple Market*, 1889).

The collection donated by Dr Eduardo Mollard, an Argentinian who had settled in France, is a major set of works that illustrates the changes that occurred in landscape painting. In accordance with Dr Mollard's wishes, the collection is presented in a room bearing his name. Jongkind, a Dutch artist trained in the tradition of seventeenth-century Dutch landscape painting was often attracted by city scenes, such as *The Seine and Notre Dame de Paris* or *Rue de l'Abbé de l'Epée* (1872), both illuminated by a vibrant light suggested by fragmented brushstrokes.

Later, a group of Dutch artists renewed the Dutch concept of landscape painting and formed the The Hague school; Jacob Maris's paintings were dominated by a high sky (*View of Rotterdam*, 1883), while Anton Mauve captured the wind, rough seas and turbulent skies in a harmony of pale greys. Hendrik Mesdag, who enjoyed seascapes, painted stormy seas from nature or tried to catch the atmosphere of a given moment *(Sunset)*.

Hendrik Willem Mesdag
1831-1915
Sunset
Oil on canvas
140 x 180 cm
Purchased in 1887

Johan Barthold Jongkind
1819-1891
The Seine and Notre Dame Cathedral
1864

Oil on canvas
42 x 56.5 cm
Enriqueta Alsop bequest,
on behalf of Dr Eduardo
Mollard, 1972

Eugène Boudin
1824-1898
Trouville Beach
1864
Oil on wood
26 x 48 cm
Dr Eduardo Mollard
donation, 1961

In the early 1860s, the Paris studio of the academic painter, Charles Gleyre, became a meeting place for young artists wanting to perfect their drawing and painting skills. Renoir first of all, in 1861, then Frédéric Bazille, from Montpellier, Claude Monet and Alfred Sisley enrolled there, and a friendship soon sprang up among these young artists, all attracted by Realism.

Obviously, their earliest works fit into a "modern" Realist stream, mingling the influences of Courbet, Daubigny and Corot, as well as that of Delacroix, whose dash and colour were much admired. Lastly, they discovered Manet's work in 1863 and his example was a precious encouragement. Bazille later met and got on well with Cézanne, who introduced him to Pissarro and Armand Guillaumin; they were all experimenting with new forms of painting and soon formed a group.

Monet's early works are painted in a realistic vein in dark tones (*Hunting Trophy,* 1862); one of his most dazzling figures is *Madame Gaudibert,* 1868, an ambitious full-length portrait of the wife of one of Monet's first admirers, which vied with the large figures presented at the Salon.

A symbol of their friendship, Renoir's portrait of *Frédéric Bazille* (1867) depicts Bazille at his easel, in a harmony of grey and beige reminiscent of Manet's work. Their friendship is also manifest in Bazille's *Portrait of Renoir*, painted in the same year, which Renoir kept throughout his lifetime. Like Bazille, Renoir tried to give fresh impetus to the theme of the male nude; here, his admiration for Manet and Courbet is evident in his broad, vigorous strokes, and his masterly rendering of fabrics and flesh (*Boy with a Cat,* 1868).

In 1863, Monet and Bazille worked together in Chailly, a village on the fringe of the Forest of Fontainebleau, both painting in the tradition of the Barbizon group. When Monet was injured, Bazille showed his immobilised friend (*The Makeshift Sickbed,* 1865) in a small, finely coloured painting that betrays Manet's influence. Bazille worked on the problem of painting figures in full sunlight; he came from Montpellier and had been struck by Courbet's frank treatment of light in *The Meeting* (1854), a famous painting which belonged to the Montpellier collector, Bruyas. *Family Reunion* (1867), accepted by the Salon in 1868, shows Bazille's great sensitivity to the hard southern light, which sharply delineates planes, accentuating contrasts and the solidity of forms. The originality of the composition and the colours reveals the importance of Manet's influence, as well as the bond between Bazille and Monet in the rendering of the light filtering through the foliage and altering the colour of clothes and soil. Unfortunately, Bazille was killed in battle at Beaune-la-Rolande in 1870, at the age of twenty-nine. Paul Guigou, who settled in Marseilles in 1854 and then moved to Paris in 1862, stayed faithful to the strong Provençal light which gives stability and permanence to his characters (*The Washerwoman,* 1860) and his landscapes (*The Gineste Road,* 1859).

Monet, who had benefited from the advice of Boudin and Jongkind and seemed to be the strongest personality in the whole group (his early work was noticed by the critics in the 1865 Salon) embarked on a *Le Déjeuner sur l'herbe* (1865-1866). This large painting (about 4.60 m x over 6 m) had been designed as a homage and challenge to Edouard Manet and was supposed to be submitted to the Salon in 1866. The overall picture is known through a study in the Pushkin Museum, Moscow, because Monet did not finish *Le Déjeuner sur l'herbe*, which he later left to a creditor in Argenteuil as surety; when he bought it back in 1884, the work had been damaged from storage in a damp cellar, and Monet cut two fragments from it. The

Frédéric Bazille
1841-1870
Family Reunion
1867
Oil on canvas
152 x 230 cm
Purchased with the
contribution of Marc
Bazille, 1905

Claude Monet
1840-1926
The Magpie
1868-1869
Oil on canvas
89 x 130 cm
Purchased in 1984

left fragment has been part of the national collections since 1957, thanks to the generosity of Georges Wildenstein, while the central fragment was added to the Musée d'Orsay's collection in March 1987. This youthful work, which orients Monet's art towards the description of contemporary life, is remarkable for its authority, firmness and mastery in the rendering of the figures, and the taste for contrasting light in a carefully studied atmosphere. Monet made Bazille pose in the Forest of Fontainebleau, working from small studies painted outdoors; he also included Courbet in his composition, openly declaring his admiration for Courbet's solid workmanship and handling of light. *Women in the Garden* (1867) is another experimental work; Monet painted it the open air, but tried to keep the spontaneity and freedom of a sketch. The sharply outlined figures and dark patches of shade fit easily into the decorative garden setting. It was refused by the jury of the 1867 Salon. Only Zola defended the work: "...the jury refused a painting he had done of women in pale summer dresses, picking flowers on a garden path; the sunlight fell straight on their dazzling white skirts; the warm shadow of a tree cut a large grey piece out of the paths and the sunlit dresses. The strangest possible effect. You really have to be ahead of your time be so bold, showing fabrics sliced in half by sun and shade, and smartly dressed women in a carefully raked garden ..."

Moreover, Monet did not have any more luck in the 1869 Salon; the jury refused one of his most important paintings; *The Magpie* (1869). A strange atmosphere

Claude Monet
1840-1926
Hôtel des Roches Noires at Trouville
1870
Oil on canvas
81 x 58 cm
Jacques Laroche donation, with a life interest, 1947; entered the museum in 1976

Paul Guigou
1834-1871
The Washerwoman
1860
Oil on canvas
81 x 59 cm
Purchased in 1901

Pierre-Auguste Renoir
1841-1919
Boy with a Cat
1868
Oil on canvas
123 x 66 cm
Purchased in 1992

Pierre-Auguste Renoir
1841-1919
Frédéric Bazille
1867
Oil on canvas
105 x 73.5 cm
Marc Bazille bequest,
1924

emanates from this ambitiously large landscape, which sparkles with light and is astonishing in its subtle variety of whites. Emptied of all human presence, it focuses on the black bird perched on a fence.

It was with Boudin, at Honfleur in 1858, that Monet started to paint from nature. *Hôtel des Roches Noires at Trouville* (1870) gives a glimpse of the leisurely life of the upper middle class in a seaside resort shortly before the Franco-Prussian War in 1870. It shows early promise of Monet's originality, as his swift, allusive style makes the flags flutter and stirs up the cloudy sky.

Claude Monet
1840-1926
Women in the Garden
1867
Oil on canvas
255 x 205 cm
Purchased in 1921

Claude Monet
1840-1926
Le Déjeuner sur l'herbe

Left-side fragment
1865-1866
Oil on canvas
418 x 150 cm
Gift from Georges
Wildenstein, 1957

Central fragment
1865-1866
Oil on canvas
248 x 217 cm
Accepted in lieu
of inheritance tax, 1987

The Franco-Prussian War in 1870 scattered most of the artists: Bazille was killed, Renoir was mobilised, Degas and Manet went to Paris, Cézanne went off to L'Estaque, Monet and Pissarro travelled to London; where they discovered the English landscape painters and their attempts to catch ephemeral effects, as well as Turner's rapid, feverish touch. It was also the period when they came in contact with the great art dealer and collector Paul Durand-Ruel, who had supported Courbet; then Manet and was to become the defender of these controversial artists, who were struggling to make ends meet. They managed to survive the hardship of these years only with the help of a small circle of art enthusiasts and critics.

Tired of being systematically rejected by the jury of the official salons, they banded together with the idea of holding free exhibitions with neither jury nor awards. The first was held in 1874, showing 165 paintings by thirty participants, including Cézanne, Monet, Degas, Sisley, Berthe Morisot, Pissarro, Renoir and Boudin. One of Monet's works, *Impression, Sunrise,* drew the sneering label of "impressionist" which has stuck to the group ever since. Further exhibitions were held in 1876, 1877, 1879, 1880, 1881, 1882 and 1886 despite defections and quarrels; Manet alone systematically refused to participate. New personalities swelled the group: Gustave Caillebotte, who exhibited in 1876, soon become one of the group's patrons. He bequeathed his collection of works by his Impressionist friends to the state in 1894. The collection included *The Dance at Moulin de la Galette* (1876), *The Swing* (1876) and *Woman Reading* (1876) by Renoir, eight Monets, including *Gare St-Lazare* (1877), *Regatta at Argenteuil* (circa 1872); seven Pissarros, including *The Red Roofs* (1877), works by Manet, Sisley, Cézanne (*Estaque,* circa 1878-1879) and Degas. In 1879, at the third Impressionist exhibition, new faces appeared: Mary Cassatt, an American friend of Degas, Albert Lebourg, and above all Gauguin who was a close friend of Pissarro. The advent of Seurat and Signac in 1886 announced a new adventure in painting.

Monet, who soon emerged as the leader of the Impressionist group, settled at Argenteuil from 1872 to 1878 and all the other members of the group, even Manet, came to join him there. Renoir, Sisley, Caillebotte and Monet painted together, stimulated by the creative atmosphere, and each developed his own style. Monet abandoned large-scale paintings and figures and devoted his time to the movements of the sky and the water, the vibration of the air, the subtle reflections and fleeting effects produced by the light. The Seine and its sailing boats was the main

Claude Monet
1840-1926
The Poppies
1873
Oil on canvas
50 x 65 cm
Etienne Moreau-Nelaton
donation, 1906

Claude Monet
  1840-1926
  Regatta at Argenteuil
  Circa 1872
  Oil on canvas
  48 x 75 cm
  Gustave Caillebotte
  bequest, 1894

Claude Monet
  1840-1926
  Gare St-Lazare
  1877
  Oil on canvas
  75.5 x 104 cm
  Gustave Caillebotte
  bequest, 1894

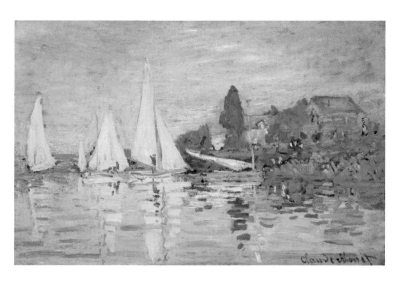

subject during this period and Monet, like Daubigny before him, frequently worked in a boat fitted out as a studio. *Regatta at Argenteuil* (circa 1872), a deliberately sketchy painting, presented a double image of reality and its reflection, whereas the fragmented brushstrokes intensified the vibrant relationship between the colours, red and green, green and blue, blue and white, and captured the effect of light glinting on the water. *The River at Argenteuil* (1872), a bright, animated painting, leaves ample room for the sky and scudding clouds, while *The Boats. Regatta at Argenteuil* (circa 1874) shows a stormy, turbulent sky, and a choppy, grey river. Renoir also painted *La Seine at Argenteuil* (circa 1873).

The Poppies (1873), which has become one of the most famous Impressionist paintings, conjures up the vibrant atmosphere of a summer's day by means of dabs of colour, while *The Railway Bridge at Argenteuil* (circa 1873), painted in quick, fragmented strokes, contrasts with the sensitive view, still close to Corot's style, that Sisley took in the same period (*Footbridge at Argenteuil*, 1872).

The Luncheon, painted by Monet about 1873, and one of the few large paintings of this period, conveys the charm of an everyday scene, the end of a family meal where we see little Jean Monet at play and a hat hung on a branch. The intimate theme and the composition seem to announce the work of Pierre Bonnard and Edouard Vuillard. Attracted by urban scenes, Monet painted seven canvases of *Gare St-Lazare* (1877), with the great locomotives smothered in whorls of blue and white smoke; six views were presented at the third Impressionist exhibition and Zola was eloquent in his praise: "Monet has exhibited superb railway stations this year. We can hear the trains rumbling in and see the smoke rolling under the immense hangars. That is painting today... Our artists must find the poetry in stations as their fathers found the poetry in forests and rivers." *Rue Montorgueil*, 1878, demonstrates Monet's skill and dazzling, joyous freedom, as with quick brushstrokes and paint he conjures up fluttering flags, crowds of people, noise and confusion.

Monet's career, like that of Renoir, continued well into the twentieth century, and reflects the different places he lived in. From 1878 to 1881 he lived at Vétheuil and strove to capture the atmosphere of the village (*Vétheuil Church, Snow*, 1878-1879; *The Seine at Vétheuil*, circa 1879-1882), especially the effects of the harsh winter of 1879-1880, the Seine frozen over and the break up of the ice.

"I am delighted. Giverny is a splendid place for me," Monet wrote in 1883, and the move marked the beginning of a new period in his career. Giverny became Monet's home port, a haven he referred to during his trips to Holland, the Normandy coast, Belle Ile in Brittany - where he painted several canvases of the sea with its "unbelievable tones" - Antibes and the Creuse. The two paintings of *Woman with a Parasol* (1886) show Monet's desire to try to portray figures outdoors once more, but he was particularly eager to catch a fleeting impression, to render the haze of light that enveloped them, and he left their features indistinct. About this time, he hit upon the idea of painting the same subject transformed by the seasons, the weather, the time of day and the changing light (*Haystacks, Late Summer*, 1890). The gift of *Effect of Wind, Poplar Series* (1891) has filled a gap in the museum's collections. Immediately after the *Haystacks* and just before the *Cathedrals*, Monet painted twenty-three pictures of the poplars planted on the left bank of the Epte River, near Giverny; he viewed them from a boat, or near the bank, seeing them from underneath, which accentuates their vertical lines and catches their graceful

Claude Monet
1840-1926
Rue Montorgueil,
National Celebration
on 30 June 1878
1878

Oil on canvas
81 x 50 cm
Accepted in lieu
of inheritance tax, 1982

movements and fluidity, translated here by curving lines and a light touch. The *Rouen Cathedral* series, painted between 1892 and 1893, although it is dated 1894, is magnificently represented at the Musée d'Orsay, which has five versions due to a generous legacy by Count Isaac de Camondo and a state purchase from the artist in 1907. Monet also made series on London, and on Vétheuil, but his later works are devoted exclusively to Giverny. These "landscapes of water and reflections" start from a study in which the composition is still clear (we can recognise the *Japanese Bridge* spanning the pond) and end up as an evocation of a floating, moving, all-encompassing world, the realm of the water lilies, which gradually extend their luxuriant, colourful presence to the entire canvas *(Blue Water Lilies,* circa 1916-1919).

Claude Monet
1840-1926
Effect of Wind, Poplar Series
1891
Oil on canvas
105 x 74 cm
Accepted in lieu
of inheritance tax, 2002

Claude Monet
1840-1926
Blue Water Lilies
Circa 1916-1919
Oil on canvas
200 x 200 cm
Purchased in 1981

Claude Monet
1840-1926
Rouen Cathedral Series
1892-1893
Oil on canvas

*The Porch and
the St Romain Tower,
Full Sun. Blue and Gold
Harmony*
107 x 73 cm
Count Isaac de Camondo
bequest, 1911

*Rouen Cathedral, the
Porch, Overcast Weather,
Grey Harmony*
100 x 65 cm
Count Isaac de Camondo
bequest, 1911

*Rouen Cathedral.
Front View of the Porch.
Brown Harmony*
107 x 73 cm
Purchased from the artist
in 1907

*The Porch and
the St Romain Tower,
Morning Effect.
White Harmony*
106 x 73 cm
Count Isaac de Camondo
bequest, 1911

*The Porch, Morning
Sun. Blue Harmony*
91 x 63 cm
Count Isaac de Camondo
bequest, 1911

Renoir sought to apply the principles of Impressionism to the study of the human figure; he painted some of his most famous pictures in his Montmartre studio – *The Dance at the Moulin de la Galette, The Swing* and *Torso of a Woman in Sunlight.* The latter drew scathing criticism and was dismissed as "a heap of rotting flesh"; Renoir had tried to render the dappled effect of sunlight filtered through foliage. The shadows range from pale pink to purple; the face seems to dissolve in the light, accentuating the dehumanisation of a model treated as a subject for study, yet it has an aura of simple sensuality that is characteristic of Renoir's work. *The Swing,* like *The Dance at the Moulin de la Galette,* shows the same preoccupations and the characters and the ground seem to quiver under the mottled patches of light and shade. Painted on the spot in an open-air café from the top of Montmartre that had been installed beside the Moulin, *The Dance at the Moulin de la Galette* caught critics off guard with its dissolving shapes and vibrant colour: "… The people are dancing on a ground like the purple clouds that darken the sky on a stormy day." Renoir excelled in portraiture and earned his living by meeting the steady demand: *Madame Charpentier,* 1876, successfully renders the elegant, worldly character of the wife of Georges Charpentier, who published the writing of Flaubert, Zola, Daudet and the Goncourt brothers. His portrait of *Claude Monet* (1875) testifies to the close friendship between the two artists. *Alphonsine Fournaise,* 1879, shown in her father's restaurant at Chatou, conjures up the noisy, friendly life along the banks of the Seine which has its literary equivalent in Guy de Maupassant's stories.

The early 1880s was a period of introspection and sometimes crisis for all the artists in the Impressionist group: the new style of painting that dissolved forms, which seems natural in Monet, was seen as a danger by Renoir and was rejected by the younger artists. Renoir spoke his mind in a letter to his art dealer Ambroise Vollard: "About 1883 there was a break in my work. I went as far as I could go in Impressionism and I came to the conclusion that I could neither paint nor draw. In short, I was at a dead end." Freed from material worries for the first time, Renoir travelled to Algeria where he luxuriated in the dazzling Mediterranean light, vivid colours and the bustling, motley crowds (*Arab Festivities in Algiers,* 1881). In Italy,

Pierre-Auguste Renoir
1841-1919
*Woman's Torso
in the Sunlight*
1876
Oil on canvas
81 x 64.8 cm
Gustave Caillebotte
bequest, 1894

Pierre-Auguste Renoir
1841-1919
Claude Monet
1875
Oil on canvas
85.6 x 60.6 cm
M. et Mme Raymond
Koechlin bequest, 1931

Pierre-Auguste Renoir
1841-1919
*Dance at Le Moulin
de la Galette*
1876
Oil on canvas
131 x 175 cm
Gustave Caillebotte
bequest, 1894

he rediscovered Raphael and the Renaissance masters he had admired as a young man in the Louvre, and visited the great sites of classical antiquity: Naples, Pompeii and Sicily. He showed fresh interest in drawing and line, which is apparent in two large paintings, *Dance in the City* and *Dance in the Country* (1883). Although they were designed as a pair, each scene has its own structure and distinct outlines; his palette is simpler and includes the acid colours typical of this period. The interest in drawing and sharp outlines is similarly in evidence in the portrait of Madame Renoir and her son Pierre (*Motherhood*, 1887). Berthe Morisot saw this painting in Renoir's studio and so admired it that she commissioned him to paint a portrait of her daughter *Julie Manet* (1887), which combines simple forms and fresh colours, giving the painting a carefully finished, almost enamelled look. In 1888, Renoir went through another period of discouragement, rejecting some of his paintings which he found too dry and developed a new manner, sometimes described as "pearly", in which line gives way to a suppler treatment and warmer colours. *Young Girls at the Piano*, which, thanks to Mallarmé's intervention, was the state's first purchase from Renoir, in 1892, is lightly painted in warm colours and infused with golden light. Another version of the same theme, in colder more strongly contrasted tones, is in the Walter-Guillaume collection (Musée de l'Orangerie, Paris).

Renoir's last masterpiece, *The Bathers* (circa 1918-1919), was painted in his home, Les Collettes at Cagnes-sur-Mer. It is an ambitious painting, enriched by memories of Rubens and the great Venetian masters; the figures are grouped in the landscape and partake of its light and warmth. Stricken with rheumatism, Renoir cried: "Now that I no longer have the use of my arms and legs, I would love to paint big canvases. I dream of nothing but Veronese, of the *Wedding at Cana*, what misery!"

Pierre-Auguste Renoir
1841-1919
Dance in the Country
1882-1883
Oil on canvas
180 x 90 cm
Purchased in 1979

Dance in the City
1883
Oil on canvas
180 x 90 cm
Accepted in lieu
of inheritance tax, 1978

Pierre-Auguste Renoir
1841-1919
Julie Manet,
or *Girl with a Cat*
1887
Oil on canvas
65.5 x 53.5 cm
Accepted in lieu
of inheritance tax, 1999

Pierre-Auguste Renoir
1841-1919
Young Girls at the Piano
1892
Oil on canvas
116 x 90 cm
Purchased by the State
from the artist, 1892

Pierre-Auguste Renoir
1841-1919
The Bathers
Circa 1918-1919
Oil on canvas
110 x 160 cm
Gift from the artist's son,
1923

Impressionism
Berthe Morisot, Gustave Caillebotte, Camille Pissarro, Alfred Sisley

Manet's sister-in-law and pupil, Berthe Morisot, participated in most of the Impressionist exhibitions. She experimented enthusiastically with outdoor painting, but continued to paint portraits and interiors. *The Cradle* (1872), shown at the first Impressionist exhibition in 1874, is harmonious and subtly coloured, fresh and luminous. *Young Woman Dressed for the Ball* (1879), a brilliant, freely painted study of a young woman in evening dress, is one of Morisot's most successful works with its vivacity and the finesse of the colours. Charles Ephrussi wrote in the *Gazette des Beaux-Arts*: "Madame Berthe Morisot is French in her distinction, elegance, gaiety and carefree style; she crushes flower petals on her palette then spreads them on the canvas in airy, spiritual strokes, tossing them rather by chance. They harmonise and combine and end up producing something fine, lively and charming that we sense rather than see."

Gustave Caillebotte, an art collector and patron, started out as a Realist, with scenes of contemporary life (*The Floor Scrapers,* 1875) or views of Paris. *The Floor Scrapers* caught the critics' eye at the second Impressionist exhibition in 1876. It is a large painting, impressively modern in its unbalanced composition, and traditional but energetic style with fine rendering of materials such as the wood shavings, the uncompromising realism of the labourers, and the quality of the light. Later, when he had retired to his house at Le Petit Gennevilliers, Caillebotte concentrated on views of the Seine. *Sailing Boats at Argenteuil* (circa 1888) reveals Monet's influence in the rendering of the light and reflections, but his accurate depiction of the boats, masts and sails indicates his attachment to the real world.

Pissarro settled in Pontoise in 1872; he presented *Hoar Frost* (1873) at the first Impressionist exhibition in 1874 and sparked a scandal. "Call those furrows? Call that frost? They are nothing but palette scrapings laid uniformly on a dirty canvas. It has neither head nor tail, nor up nor down, nor front nor back." The baldness of the subject disconcerted the critics; indeed, Pissarro had left out all picturesque or anecdotal details, and concentrated on capturing the gleam of sunlight on the soil and in the sky. *Hermitage Hill, Pontoise* (1873) harmoniously balances a light touch, refined colours and a firm structure, the same approach as taken by Cézanne who, at the time, was painting alongside him. Pissarro's friendship with the painter Ludovic Piette gave him an opportunity to paint at Montfoucault in Mayenne. *Harvest at Montfoucault* (1876), broadly executed with both the brush and the palette knife in a delicate range of colours, contrasts with *The Red Roofs,* whose solid composition recalls the early landscapes at the Hermitage, with thick paint and rich colour.

Antonin Personnaz (1854-1936), a native of Bayonne like the painter Léon Bonnat, was introduced into the Parisian art world by Bonnat. He made friends with Pissarro, Degas and Guillaumin and, from 1880, built up a collection rich in Impressionist works. After the First World War, he retired to Bayonne where he helped manage the Musée Bonnat and watched over the art works that his friend had left to the city. Personnaz bequeathed his collection of paintings, pastels, watercolours and drawings to the national museums (apart from about forty works which are in the Musée Bonnat), and it was exhibited at the Louvre in 1937. Pissarro is certainly one of the best represented artists and the collection follows the development of his work from 1870 to 1902. Attracted by the earth and country landscapes, living first at Louveciennes, then Pontoise, where Cézanne joined him, Pissarro shows a remarkable talent for firm execution and composition and a rich palette

Berthe Morisot
1841-1895
The Cradle
1872
Oil on canvas
56 x 46 cm
Purchased in 1930

Camille Pissarro
1830-1903
Hoar Frost
1873
Oil on canvas
65 x 93 cm
Enriqueta Alsop bequest
on behalf of Dr Eduardo
Mollard, 1972

Gustave Caillebotte
1848-1894
The Floor Scrapers
1875
Oil on canvas
102 x 146.5 cm
Purchased in 1896

Mary Cassatt
1844-1926
Young Girl in the Garden
circa 1880-1882
Oil on canvas
92 x 63 cm

dominated by brown, green and red (*Winter Landscape at Louveciennes,* circa 1870). In the 1880s, Pissarro, too, was wracked by doubt. Although he had mainly been a landscape painter, he gave new importance to the human figure which dominated his work in these years. *Girl with a Stick* (1881) is one of the first canvases testifying to his renewed interest in figure painting, and the landscape is no more than a background. The composition is both structured and sensitive, the brush strokes are sometimes fine and sometimes thick, an indication of Pissarro's research. *Young Peasant Woman Lighting a Fire. White Frost* (1887-1888), an ambitious painting, seems to consolidate this new direction and highlights the complexity of his technique, a series of tight comma-shaped strokes, enlivened by the experience of the Neo-Impressionists, which gives his canvas a clear composition and a gentle, even luminosity. The paint is dense and the colours – blue, vermilion, orange, green and yellow with touches of white – give a warm, mild autumnal tone to the whole. From 1884 to 1903, Pissarro lived at Eragny-sur-Epte. Curious by nature and forever on the lookout for new techniques, he adopted the pointillism developed by Seurat and Signac in 1885-1886 (*Woman in an Enclosure,* 1887) but soon branched into a suppler, more luminous style to paint the streets of Paris, Rouen and Dieppe (*Dieppe, Duquesne Basin,* 1902).

Alfred Sisley, a British citizen living in France, was strongly attracted to the landscape of the Ile de France region. He settled in the outskirts of Paris, between Louveciennes and Marly, and painted roads cutting into the landscape (*Chemin de la Machine, Louveciennes,* 1873), a subject that had already inspired Corot, or the melancholic tranquillity of a village transformed by a sheet of water or a cloudy, grey sky (*Flood at Port Marly,* 1876). *Snow at Louveciennes* (1878) has the balance, discretion and sensitivity typical of Sisley's art. He moved to Moret-sur-Loing in 1880, and focused mainly on painting views of the village. *Moret Bridge,* 1893, is a good illustration of his use of a monumental composition to render a quiet, familiar place.

Friendly with Cézanne and Pissarro, Armand Guillaumin executed a number of refined urban landscapes in pale colours (*Charenton Port,* 1878; *La Place Valhubert,* circa 1875). The collection bequeathed Van Gogh's last friend Dr Gachet, added to that of Antonin Personnaz, shows Signac's influence in Guillaumin's increasing use of vivid colours.

Mary Cassatt, an American painter living in France, was befriended and advised by Degas; her favourite subjects were the human figure and the faithful portrayal of everyday activities (*Young Girl in the Garden,* circa 1880-1882).

Alfred Sisley
1839-1899
Flood at Port Marly
1876
Oil on canvas
60 x 81 cm
Count Isaac de Camondo
bequest, 1911

Camille Pissarro
1830-1903
The Shepherdess or *Girl
with a Stick; Seated
Peasant Girl*
1881

Oil on canvas
81 x 64.7 cm
Count Isaac de Camondo
bequest, 1911

Camille Pissarro
1830-1903
The Red Roofs
1877

Oil on canvas
54.5 x 65.6 cm
Gustave Caillebotte
bequest, 1894

From the very beginning Degas was in a class of his own, an utterly original artist who used the old masters (Italian Renaissance painters) and great modern painters (Ingres) as a springboard for his own highly individual style. After studying under Lamothe, a disciple of Hippolyte Flandrin, Degas stayed from 1856 to 1859 in Italy, where part of his family was living. He made friends with other French artists there, such as Gustave Moreau. His youthful works are mostly portraits, such as that of his grandfather *Hilaire de Gas* (1857), then aged 87 and living in Naples. The painting already reveals his strict construction, perfect draughtsmanship, psychological insight, and skilled use of light to bring out the character of his model. In the later portrait of *Thérèse de Gas* (1863), the artist's beloved sister, the shy, serious image of the girl in a grey dress with her big black shawl and hat tied with a pink bow, is an opportunity for a magnificent piece of painting.

Preceded by a large number of studies or sketches, and surprising in its format, *The Bellelli Family* (circa 1858-1860) was begun by Degas when he was staying with his aunt, Baroness Bellelli, in Florence. This monumental set of portraits in an interior, simply composed but enriched with perspectives glimpsed though a door or in a mirror, and painted in sober but refined colours (a play of black and white) is also the portrayal of the family drama played out between Laure Bellelli and her husband, in which we can see Degas' taste for psychological studies. Despite all the influences hidden in this work (Holbein or Van Dyck for instance), *The Bellelli Family* cannot be compared to any known painting at the time.

The unfinished, mysterious *Semiramis Building Babylon* (1861) testifies to Degas' originality as a history painter. This painting reveals the artist's admiration for Italian painting of the Quattrocento, and can be compared to Piero della Francesca's murals at Arezzo. The hieratic poses, the frieze structure, the tranquil yet heroic mood, and the legendary architecture all conjure up an imaginative, poetic world where time seems to stand still. From the end of the 1860s, Degas turned

Edgar Degas
1834-1917
Semiramis Building Babylon
1861
Oil on canvas
151 x 258 cm
Purchased in 1918

Edgar Degas
1834-1917
The Bellelli Family
Circa 1858-1860
Oil on canvas
200 x 250 cm
Purchased in 1918

Edgar Degas
1834-1917
The Absinthe Drinkers
1876
Oil on canvas
92 x 68 cm
Count Isaac de Camondo
bequest, 1911

Edgar Degas
1834-1917
The Stock Exchange
Circa 1878-1879
Oil on canvas
100 x 82 cm
Purchased in 1879

to the themes he favoured in his mature years, the opera and the races (*The Parade,* also known as *Racehorses in Front of the Stands,* circa 1866-68).

"No art has as little spontaneity as mine. What I do is the result of much thought and careful study of the old masters." Degas' genius lay in giving the feeling of catching the instantaneity of the real world, through exacting experimentation and rigorous construction. He constantly reworked his pictures, insisting on line and drawing to define form. Always unsatisfied, endlessly searching for perfection, he remained an independent artist, refusing to devote his time solely to outdoor painting or the obsession with catching changes in light, as the Impressionists did, although he exhibited his work with them and shared their ideas on the freedom of painting.

"You need a natural life, the artificial life is for me," he explained to Pissarro; attracted by Baudelaire's "modernity" and by unusual subjects, Degas focused on the lively environment of the racecourse or the closed world of the Opera House, both pretexts for a detailed study of movement, and asymmetrical, original compositions. Like Manet, whom he met at the Louvre, Degas was interested in the café culture: *Absinthe Drinkers* (1876), apart from its naturalist theme, which reveals an aspect of popular life that Zola explored in his novels (*L'Assommoir – Drunkard*), shows Degas' inventiveness in the representation of space, which he suggests rather than constructs, by means of an off-centre composition, and the shifting perspective used for the tables in the foreground.

The ballet world is viewed from above (*Rehearsal of a Ballet on Stage,* 1874), or in an accelerated, vanishing perspective (*Dance Class,* 1873-75/1876), or in a space animated and diversified by doors and mirrors (*Dance Foyer at the Opera House,* 1872). It gave Degas an opportunity to use a colourful, sometimes acid palette, and to take a lucid, ironic look backstage at ballerinas at rest, weary, stretching, scratching their backs or standing in ungainly poses. After 1880, he concentrated increasingly on colour in his paintings and pastels; colour gradually modelled form, complementing the role of drawing and line and eventually replacing it. This can be seen in *Blue Dancers* (circa 1893) in which bold framing, the sparkling effect of artificial lighting expressed by touches of blue, green, yellow and pink, and the intense colours conjure up the feverish excitement of a magical world.

Racecourses were another of his favourite haunts, giving him an excuse to render the bright sheen of the jockeys' silks, the colour of the horses and their glossy,

Edgar Degas
1834-1917
Racehorses before the Stands
Circa 1879
Oil on canvas
46 x 61 cm
Count Isaac de Camondo bequest, 1911

Edgar Degas
1834-1917
Blue Dancers
Circa 1893
Oil on canvas
85 x 75.5 cm
Gift from Dr and Mrs
Albert Charpentier, 1951

damp coats and movement arrested at the point of disequilibrium. Degas was also a shrewd observer of the bourgeoisie, portrayed at work (*The Stock Exchange*, circa 1878-1879) or in their homes (*Madame Jeantaud at the Mirror*, circa 1874), and the working class in their workshops – milliners or ironing women. *The Ironers*, circa 1884-1886, explored a theme that had earlier been treated by Daumier. Degas used a synthetic style, entering into a direct relation with the canvas itself, leaving parts blank, and using muted colours to suggest a grey, damp atmosphere.

Skilled in all techniques – oil, lead pencil, black chalk, watercolour and charcoal – Degas enriched the use of pastel by mixing it with other media. Gouache, distemper, and oil thinned with turpentine were combined with coloured crayon and pastel became a rich, transparent, profound medium which Degas used for monotypes (a drawing on a plate, usually in oils, yielding a single print on paper).

Pastel became increasingly important in Degas' work: in 1869, after a stay in Boulogne, he painted a series of seascapes. In the quiet of his studio he recreated his impressions of the sea, building up the atmosphere and suggesting shapes (*Cliffs by the Sea; Seascape*). From 1873 to 1878 he focused more on Paris night life, with its cafés and brothels, and evenings at the ballet or the opera. Although sometimes shown at rest (*Seated Dancer*, circa 1881-1883), Degas' dancers are usually caught in mid-air or in a pirouette (*The Star or Dancer on Stage*, 1878), as he tries to seize the instantaneity of a fleeting movement (*End of an Arabesque*, circa 1877) in flamboyant, iridescent colours. The effect is heightened by an off-centre composition, abrupt cropping, and harsh or mysterious lighting. The very large pastel *Dancers* (circa 1884-1885), given to the museum in 1997, has a special place in the artist's oeuvre. He simplified the composition, using an almost square canvas, grouped his figures together, whitened their tutus to blend them with the dancers' bodies, and by alternating thick layers of pastel with light strokes which let the paper show through, gave the grey, dusty impression of a dreary room. It is a unique masterpiece which gave rise to neither variations nor replicas.

At the last Impressionist exhibition, in 1886, Degas exhibited a set of pastels entitled: *Series of Female Nudes Bathing, Washing and Drying Themselves, Combing their Hair or Having it Combed*. We find the same techniques as in his studies of dancers: different viewpoints, multiple perspectives, foreshortening, varied and carefully controlled lighting, enriched by the use of unusual tonalities which enhance the velvety texture of flesh. *The Tub* (1886) is one of the finest examples. Degas also used hatching and vertical strokes of pastel to bring out the luminosity and shapes of the bodies (*Woman Drying the Nape of her Neck, After Her Bath*, 1898; *After the Bath*, circa 1895-1898). *At the Milliner's* (circa 1898) is the culmination of one of Degas' favourite series, which he had begun in 1879.

Edgar Degas
1834-1917
*The Ballerina or Dancer
on the Stage*
circa 1876-1877

Pastel on monotype
60 x 44 cm
Bequest by Gustave
Caillebotte, 1894

Edgar Degas
1834-1917
Dancers
Circa 1884-1885
Pastel
75 x 73 cm
Accepted in lieu
of inheritance tax, 1997

Edgar Degas
1834-1917
The Tub
1886
Pastel sur carton
600 x 830 cm
Count Isaac de Camondo
bequest, 1911

Post-impressionism
Paul Cézanne

"The artist who has been the most fiercely attacked and mistreated by the press and the public over the last fifteen years is Mr Cézanne. There is no outrageous epithet that has not been stuck on his name, and his works have provoked gales of laughter which still echo today," wrote Georges Rivière after the third Impressionist exhibition in 1877, the last in which Cézanne participated. The letters Cézanne exchanged with his few friends and admirers give a glimpse of the loneliness of an artist assailed by constant doubts. When Emile Zola published *L'Oeuvre* in 1886, Cézanne saw himself in the novel's hero, Claude Lantier, described as "a failed genius", a "self-destructive intelligence". Despite the dreams and hopes they had shared, he broke off his friendship with Zola, whom he had known since their childhood days in Aix-en-Provence.

In 1861, Cézanne told his father, a banker in Aix-en-Provence, that he wanted to paint. The portraits of his uncle Dominique (*Uncle Dominique as a Lawyer,* circa 1866) make use of new technical solutions: the canvas is covered with a thick layer of paint spread with a knife, which enabled the artist to render the relief, volume and intensity of the colour without using chiaroscuro, relying solely on the violence of the paint itself. His early works show the influence of the old and modern masters he had seen in the Louvre: the lessons of the Venetian painters and Caravaggio are perceptible in *Mary Magdalene* (circa 1868-1869), whose prostrate body, grieving pose and dramatic intensity are reinforced by the use of forcefully spread dark colours. *Pastoral or Idyll* (1870), a subject which Cézanne explored more fully later, testifies to the same sources, tempered by Romanticism and the modernity of Manet's *Déjeuner sur l'herbe. Achille Emperaire* (circa 1868), a caricature of one of Cézanne's friends, a crippled painter from Aix, was rejected by the Salon in 1870. At the first Impressionist exhibition, *A Modern Olympia* (circa 1873-1874) triggered a hail of jibes; it was an erotic, theatrical interpretation of Manet's painting, which reveals Cézanne's evolution towards luminous colour and a brilliant execution. During his stay in Auvers, he painted a series of still lifes, a theme that he explored throughout his lifetime, and has here treated in a realistic manner (*Green Apples,* circa 1873; *Bouquet with the Little Delft Vase,* circa 1873*)*.

In 1872, Cézanne moved to Auvers-sur-Oise to be near Pissarro, working alongside and strongly influenced by the older man. *The House of the Hanged Man* (1873), with its fragmented brushstrokes, pale colours and simple motif, reveals Pissarro's influence, but the sturdy structure and the desire for a rigorous spatial framework are Cézanne's own contribution. But it was in *The Gulf of Marseilles seen from L'Estaque* that he asserted his concept of space and perspective; the landscape is divided into three broad zones, sharply delineated by the contrast in colour. *Maincy Bridge* (1879), painted during a sojourn in Melun, marked his definitive break with Impressionism, for it depicted a timeless landscape. The desire to fit figures into a landscape, which can be seen in his work from 1870 onwards, became an obsession with Cézanne over the years. Over and over again, in oils or watercolour, he came back to the same postures, inspired by drawings and sculptures, and gradually moved towards a lyrical style exalting man's harmony with nature, expressed in a range of blues and greens. Volumes and spaces were closely intertwined. These works had a considerable influence on young artists such as Maurice Denis, Henri Matisse and Pablo Picasso, who each owned a version of the *Bathers* (*Bathers,* 1890-1900 belonged to Maurice Denis).

Paul Cézanne
1839-1906
The Card Players
Circa 1890-1895
Oil on canvas
47.5 x 57 cm
Count Isaac de Camondo
bequest, 1911

Paul Cézanne
1839-1906
L'Estaque
Circa 1878-1879
Oil on canvas
59.5 x 73 cm
Gustave Caillebotte
bequest, 1894

Paul Cézanne
1839-1906
Apples and Oranges
Circa 1895-1900
Oil on canvas
74 x 93 cm
Count Isaac de Camondo
bequest, 1911

Paul Cézanne
1839-1906
Gustave Geffroy
(1855-1926)
1895
Oil on canvas
110 x 89 cm
Donation with a life
interest from the grand-
daughter of Auguste
Pellerin, 1969;
entered the museum
in 2000

Paul Cézanne
1839-1906
Woman with a Coffee Pot
Circa 1890-1895
Oil on canvas
130 x 96.5 cm
Gift from Mr and Mrs
Jean-Victor Pellerin, 1956

Paul Cézanne
1839-1906
Portrait of the Artist
against a Pink Background
circa 1875
Oil on canvas
66 x 55 cm
Anonymous donation to
the French state on
condition of usufruct,
2000

The closed world of *The Card Players* (circa 1890-1895) is a pretext for a study of lines and volumes. Of the five paintings that Cézanne devoted to this theme, this is plainly the version in which the tension between shapes and characters is at its height. The painted study of a *Card Player* confirms his gradual approach to the subject. His monumental *Woman with a Coffee Pot* (circa 1890-1895) is treated like a still life, stripped of emotion and feelings; it gives an insight into Cézanne's growing tendency to give the body as geometrical forms and to "see nature in terms of cylinders, spheres and cones." When the life interest on the donation made by Auguste Pellerin's granddaughter came to an end in 2000, two major works entered the collection: *Montagne Sainte Victoire* (circa 1890) and *Portrait of Gustave Geffroy* (1895-1896), a writer and art critic portrayed at his desk in a feverish whirl of light and colour. A major donation to the state in 2000, subject to a life interest, brought two other outstanding works to the museum: *Still Life with an Open Drawer* (1877-1879), and *Portrait of the Artist against a Pink Background* (circa 1875) which greatly impressed the poet Rainer Maria Rilke at the Salon d'Automne in 1907; he commented on "the powerful structure of this skull modelled from the inside... the incredible intensity ... and the grandeur, the incorruptibility of this impartial gaze."

Still lifes were a favourite subject from the start of Cézanne's career. *The Blue Vase* (circa 1885-1887) reveals one of his major interests: the study of light on objects and colours, the construction of space through the interplay of vertical and horizontal lines. Later, he took a different perspective and showed objects from a high viewpoint or from several viewpoints at once (*Apples and Oranges,* 1895-1900).

Paul Cézanne
1839-1906
*Achille Emperaire
(1829-1898)*
Circa 1868
Oil on canvas
200 x 120 cm
Gift from Mrs René
Lecomte, 1964

Paul Cézanne
1839-1906
Bathers
Circa 1890-1892
Oil on canvas
60 x 82 cm
Donation from Baroness
Eva Gebhard-Gourgaud,
1965

Post-impressionism
Vincent Van Gogh

Vincent Van Gogh's life and work are inextricably intertwined, and each journey he made, whether freely chosen or driven by his anguished temperament, shaped a new period and prompted fresh artistic experiments. He was born the son of a pastor in the province of Brabant and it was not until 1880, after his failure as a preacher, that he turned to painting.

His early career – his Dutch period – is characterised by dark, thickly painted canvases of peasants from Borinage, the mining district of Belgium where he had tried to work as a pastor. In 1886, Van Gogh moved to Paris, where his brother Théo was already living and working for the art dealer Adolphe Goupil. Theo's strong affection and financial and moral support were constant throughout the painter's short life. Vincent confided in his brother, recounting all the details of his life and his painting in a copious, moving and sometimes heartrending correspondence. His contacts with Pissarro, Signac, Gauguin, Emile Bernard and Toulouse-Lautrec had a decisive influence on Van Gogh's work; he borrowed light and colour from the Impressionists (*Restaurant de la Sirène,* 1877). He was a regular customer at Le Tambourin, a cabaret in the Boulevard de Clichy, and even put on an exhibition there; *The Italian Woman* (1887) – probably Agostina Segatori, the owner of the cabaret – is a slightly off-centre, highly simplified portrait, with neither shadows nor perspective, vigorously brushed in blocks of intense colour.

In February 1888, Vincent set off for Arles where he revelled in the light and warmth of southern France; colour and synthetic design are the most striking features of his works during this period. Interested in portraiture, Van Gogh used his landlady, Madame Ginoux (*L'Arlésienne*) as a model: "... At last I have found an Arlesienne ... pale lemon background, grey face, black, black, black clothing, raw

Vincent Van Gogh
1853-1890
Self-Portrait
1889
Oil on canvas
65 x 54.5 cm
Gift from Paul and
Marguerite Gachet, 1949

Vincent Van Gogh
1853-1890
Church at Auvers-sur-Oise
1890
Oil on canvas

94 x 74.5 cm
Purchased with the contribution of Paul Gachet and an anonymous Canadian donation, 1951

Vincent Van Gogh
1853-1890
Doctor Gachet (1828-1909)
1890
Oil on canvas
68 x 57 cm
Gift from Paul and Marguerite Gachet, 1949

Vincent Van Gogh
1853-1890
Starry Night
Arles, 1888
Oil on canvas
72.5 x 92 cm
Donation with a life interest from Mr and Mrs Robert Kahn-Sriber In memory of Mr and Mrs Fernand Moch, 1975; entered the museum in 1995

Prussian blue. She is sitting in an orange wooden armchair with her elbows on a green table." Vincent urged Gauguin, whose art he passionately admired, to join him in Arles. *The Dance Hall in Arles,* (1888), reveals the influence of Gauguin and Bernard, both pioneers of Synthetism and Cloisonnism. Shapes here are outlined, enclosed as if in a stained glass window, and the areas of bright solid colour brushed with a violence that caricatures and distorts the faces. With broad strokes of cobalt blue, he created a visionary *Starry Night over the Rhône* (1888), the darkness illuminated by the gas lamps, and the Great Bear constellation filling the canvas with luxuriant, glowing stars. A sense of infinity emanates from the scene and the two human shapes seem utterly alienated from the power and mystery of the world... The break-up of his friendship with Gauguin, whom Van Gogh tried to injure at the end of 1889, drove him to slash his left ear in a bout of madness, then commit himself to the hospital in Saint-Rémy. While there he painted another version of his *Bedroom in Arles* (1889), a whirl of colour and motion. His *Self-Portrait* in 1889 is one of the last of a series in which Van Gogh anxiously scrutinised his own image; the face is set against a pale, floating, palpitating, wavy background but it also reveals perfect self-control and total lucidity about his attacks. *Noon* or *Rest From Work* (1889-1890), after an engraving of a drawing by Millet, also dates from his hospitalisation in Saint-Rémy; it is a calm, luminous picture, which in Van Gogh's words "tries to translate into another language, the language of colour, the black-and-white impressions of chiaroscuro."

After a short stay in Paris, Van Gogh moved to Auvers-sur-Oise on the invitation of Dr Gachet, who treated and befriended him, and above all admired, respected and accepted his painting. Vincent painted three portraits of *Doctor Gachet;* in the process, he wrote to Théo: "I am working on his portrait, the head in a white cap, very blond, very pale, the hands pale, too, a blue dress coat and a cobalt blue background, leaning on a red table which has a yellow book and a purple foxglove on it." Dr Gachet moved in artistic circles and had made friends with many of the Impressionists; he invited Guillaumin, Pissarro and Cézanne to Auvers and bought some of their paintings (now in the Musée d'Orsay, in the Personnaz collection and the Cézanne room). Van Gogh's 1889 *Self-Portrait, Portrait of Doctor Gachet* (1890) and *The Church at Auvers* (1890) are some of the finest works in his collection, part of which was most generously donated to the state by his children, Paul and Marguerite, in 1954. The agitated, spinning forms of *The Church at Auvers,* with its "expressive, sumptuous" colour, show the peaceful village church in a violent, dramatic light; this oppressive nocturnal anxiety, expressed by colour and volumes, is not unlike the visions of the Norwegian painter Edvard Munch.

Desperately lonely and distressed, Van Gogh took a revolver and shot himself; he died on 29 July 1890.

Vincent Van Gogh
1853-1890
Van Gogh's Bedroom in Arles
1889

Oil on canvas
57.5 x 74 cm
Entered the museum in application of the peace treaty with Japan, 1959

Vincent Van Gogh
1853-1890
Siesta
1889-1890
Oil on canvas

73 x 91 cm
Donation from
Mrs Fernand Halphen
with a life interest, 1952;
entered the museum
in 1963

Vincent Van Gogh
1853-1890
The Arlesienne
1888
Oil on canvas
92.3 x 73.5 cm
Donation with a life
interest from Mrs R de
Goldschmidt Rothschild,
Announced in
August 1944; entered
the museum in 1974

Neo-Impressionism
Georges Seurat, Paul Signac, Henri-Edmond Cross

The term "Neo-Impressionism" was used for the first time in Félix Fénéon's report on the eighth Impressionist exhibition in 1886. Georges Seurat, who was the originator of the new technique, showed *Sunday at La Grande Jatte* (1884-1886, Chicago, Art Institute); but he had already astonished people with *Bathing, Asnières* (1883-1884, London, Tate Gallery), which was rejected by the jury of the official Salon, and presented at the first Salon des Indépendants in 1884. Both works are evoked in the Musée d'Orsay by small, rapid sketches.

Also known as Pointillism or Divisionism, the technique invented by Seurat consisted in laying dots of separate colours side by side on the canvas to reinforce the richness, solidity and brilliance of the tones; the spectator's eye mixes the pigments and recreates the colours. This approach is both a continuation of Delacroix's experiments, which were further developed by the Impressionists, and an application of treatises on colour by scientists such as Michel-Eugène Chevreul and Charles Blanc. Before fully mastering his technique, Seurat made several studies in the open air; one such study is *Peasant Boy in Blue* (circa 1882), a monumental, imposing figure despite his diminutive size. Three highly elaborate studies for *The Models* (1888, Barnes Foundation, Merion, Pennsylvania) offer an introduction to Seurat's compact world; we see the same nude model in three different poses; she seems to be made of nothing but air and light, but her shape does not disappear altogether (*Standing Model; Seated Model from the Side; Model from the Back*, 1886).

Seurat spent the summer of 1888 at Port-en-Bessin, a village on the Normandy coast discovered by his friend Signac. He brought back a group of landscapes: *Por-en-Bessin* (1888) plays on coloured rhythms and lines – the horizontal lines of the wharves, the curves of the cliffs – and leaves the main part of the canvas to the sea and the sky in a calm, poetic mood. The dotted border, like the border around the *Models*, was added by the artist to ensure a harmonious transition from

Georges Seurat
1859-1891
Model from the Back
1886-1887
Oil on wood
24.5 x 15.5 cm
Purchased in 1977

Georges Seurat
1859-1891
The Circus
1891
Oil on canvas
185.5 x 152.5 cm
John Quinn bequest, 1924

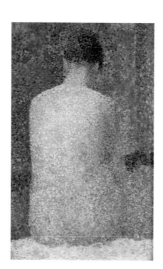

Georges Seurat
1859-1891
Port-en-Bessin,
Port at High Tide
1888

Oil on canvas
67 x 82 cm
Purchased with the back
interest on an anonymous
Canadian donation, 1952

the canvas to the frame. His last work, the unfinished *Circus* (1891), has a strange feeling, suggesting the gaiety and excitement of the show by rising streaks of red and yellow (for the ring and the circus performers), while the spectators are placed on the horizontal lines of the tiered seats suggesting calmness and stability in an overall tonality of yellow and purple. It echoes Charles Henry's theories on the dynamics of lines. The flat, simplified outlines, the curving arabesques, all reveal an overriding concern for decoration (a small oil study helps us see how the painting developed). Around Seurat, other artists – Signac, Cross, Charles Angrand and Albert Dubois-Pillet – applied the Divisionist technique, each with his own temperament and sensibility.

Signac initially followed the Impressionists (*The Road to Gennevilliers*, 1883) and then actively experimented with Divisionism; after Seurat's death, he went south to Saint-Tropez and Antibes. *Women at the Well* (1892) and its numerous preparatory sketches, in dazzling colours with the curving, flowing lines peculiar to Art Nouveau, is an illustration of the Pointillist theory taken to the extreme. However, *The Red Buoy* (1895), liberated from the strictures of scientific theory, is painted in broader strokes while its bright colours are fragmented in a myriad of reflections. *Château des Papes* (1900), confirms the use of brushstrokes "in proportion to the size of the painting", which made his canvases look like mosaics (*The Entrance to the Port of La Rochelle*, 1921), and his increasing care with light and colour. Cross painted harmonious, pure pictures, such as *The Golden Isles* (1891), a colourful, almost abstract variation. His large landscapes are sometimes tinged with the Idealism of Puvis de Chavannes and the Nabis (*The Evening Air*, 1893-1894) or used as a pretext for exalting colour (*Cypresses at Cagnes*, 1908). On the contrary, Maximilien Luce's Realism inspired him to paint scenes from everyday life (*Quai*

Paul Signac
1863-1935
The Red Ball
1895
Oil on canvas
81 x 65 cm
Donation from Dr Pierre
Hébert with a life interest,
1957;
entered the museum
in 1973

Maximilien Luce
1858-1941
*Quai St Michel and Notre
Dame Cathedral*
1901
Oil on canvas
73 x 60 cm
Gift from Christian
Humann through the
Lutece Foundation, 1981

Henri Edmond Cross
1856-1910
Evening Air
1893-1894
Oil on canvas
115.6 x 163.2 cm

Donation from
Mrs Ginette Signac with
a life interest, 1976;
life interest waived, 1979

Georges Lemmen
1865-1916
Aline Maréchal
1892
Oil on canvas
60 x 51 cm
Purchased in 1984

Neo-Impressionism
Georges Seurat, Paul Signac, Henri-Edmond Cross

Saint-Michel and Notre Dame). Signac made friends with a number of Belgian artists, Théo van Rysselberghe (*Sailing Boats and Estuary,* circa 1892-1893; *The Helmsman,* 1892), and Georges Lemmen, members of the active XX group, which advocated Impressionist theories. Lemmen produced his first Neo-Impressionist paintings about 1898 and his debt to Seurat is clear both in his colour range and the carefully dotted borders (*Aline Maréchal*), although some paintings show a greater concern for decoration and the flowing lines derived from Art Nouveau (*Beach at Heist,* 1891). In 1899, Signac published the core work on Divisionism, *D'Eugène Delacroix au néo-impressionnisme,* leaving the Fauves, the Cubists and the abstract painters a legacy that would launch them into new adventures.

Henri Matisse is believed to have begun *Luxe, calme et volupté* while he was staying with Signac at Saint-Tropez in summer 1904. A line from Baudelaire's *L'invitation au voyage* inspired this paradisiacal vision of a Golden Age already evoked by Puvis de Chavannes and Cross and admired in Signac's *Evening Air.* This theme owes much to the Bacchanals, Rural Concerts and Pastorals of the great Venetian painters and Poussin, and to modern versions of *Déjeuner sur l'herbe.* Before the great innovations of *The Joy of Life,* 1906, Matisse freely interpreted the ideas of Neo-Impressionism and used the bright colour range later found in his Fauvist works.

Théo van Rysselberghe
1862-1926
Sailing Boats and Estuary
Circa 1892-1893
Oil on canvas
50 x 61 cm
Purchased in 1982

Henri Matisse
1869-1954
Luxe, calme et volupté
1904
Oil on canvas
98 x 118 cm

Accepted in lieu of
inheritance tax, 1982
(on loan from the Musée
National d'Art Moderne)

Henri de Toulouse-Lautrec came from an old aristocratic family for whom drawing was a regular pastime; after two accidents that left him an invalid, painting assumed a primordial role in his life. In 1882, he studied in the studios of Bonnat, then Fernand Cormon, and in 1884 he moved to Montmartre, where he painted scenes of contemporary Parisian life. He loved the theatre and painted a portrait of the actor *Henry Samary* (1889) from the Comédie Française, unexpectedly shown on stage. Paris nightlife and the world of show business fascinated him, whether at the circus or the cabaret. "Not caring a fig for fashion, Lautrec has his own Olympia," including *Jane Avril* (1892), one of his favourite models. He designed several posters starring Jane, emphasising the movement of her legs in an elegant silhouette, firmly drawn with a flowing line which captures the strange charm of her slightly absentminded air. The incisive design and the off-centre layout characteristic of his work betray his admiration for Japanese art. Clever, arbitrary cropping portrays the *Clown Cha-U-Kao* (1895) without showing her face. His drawing is almost a snapshot, catching the clown in the act of adjusting her spiralling yellow collar in a violent harmony of colour.

In 1895, the celebrated dancer from the Moulin Rouge, La Goulue, asked Toulouse-Lautrec to decorate the booth she had rented at the Foire du Trône to present her new show, the Moorish dance of the Almehs. When the booth was sold in 1896, the two canvases changed hands often and finally reappeared in 1926 in the gallery of a dealer who had unwittingly cut them into eight fragments; they were then bought by the state. They show Lautrec's favourite models (Jane Avril and her outlandish hat) and familiar figures (Oscar Wilde and the critic Fénéon), rendered with Lautrec's caricatural verve.

"A model is always a stuffed skin. These women are alive." *Woman Pulling on her Stocking* (1894) and *Woman from Behind: Weariness* (1896) are elliptical notes

Henri de Toulouse-Lautrec
1864-1901
Jane Avril Dancing
Circa 1892
Oil on cardboard
85.5 x 45 cm
Antonin Personnaz
bequest, 1937

Henri de Toulouse-Lautrec
1864-1901
The Clown Cha-U-Kao
1895
Oil on cardboard
64 x 49 cm
Count Isaac de Camondo
bequest, 1911

sketched from life in the brothel. Lautrec made a series of lithographs of them, published in his album *Elles*. *Alone* (1896) is a synthetic image of loneliness and distress, showing the artist's desire to track down beauty in sordid surroundings... *Woman at her Toilette* (1896) follows on from Degas' work, both in its subject matter and in its accelerated perspectives.

"Nothing exists but the figure," said Lautrec, who did away with all but the most significant accessories. His friend *Paul Leclerc* (1897) one of the founders of the *Revue Blanche*, talked of Lautrec's "prodigious ease in his work" and remembers that he had posed no more than two or three hours for his portrait. Lautrec strove to express the personality of his model and has skilfully rendered his relaxed pose. He died prematurely at the age of thirty seven, leaving an abundant, unusual oeuvre which had a deep influence on the Expressionists and Picasso.

Henri de Toulouse-Lautrec
1864-1901
Panel for La Goulue's
booth at the Foire
du Trône, Paris,
Moorish Dance
or *The Almehs*
1895
Oil on canvas
285 x 307.5 cm
Purchased in 1929

Henri de Toulouse-Lautrec
1864-1901
Panel for La Goulue's
booth at the Foire
du Trône, Paris,
*Dance at the Moulin
Rouge (La Goulue and
Boneless Valentin)*
1895
Oil on canvas
298 x 316 cm
Purchased in 1929

Henri de Toulouse-
Lautrec
1864-1901
Woman at her Toilette
1896
Oil on cardboard
67 x 54 cm
Pierre Goujon bequest, 1914

Henri Rousseau
known as Le Douanier
Rousseau
1844-1910
Portrait of a Woman
Circa 1897
Oil on canvas
198 x 115 cm
Donation from Baroness
Eva Gebhard-Gourgaud,
1965

The ordinary, rather insecure life of Henri Rousseau, a customs officer in Paris – hence the nickname 'Le Douanier' – contrasts with the strange world and original style of his painting. Although he belonged to much the same generation as the Impressionists, Rousseau has a place of his own in the history of painting at the turn of the century.

He was first a self-taught, amateur artist, and retired from his job in 1893 to devote his time to painting. He openly admired the official masters, Cabanel; William Bouguereau and Gérôme, and had little affinity with Impressionism and modern trends. Through Signac's influence, he exhibited in the Salon des Indépendants in 1886, and continued to do so until his death. In 1905, he figured in the Salon d'Automne among the Fauves. *War* (1894), presented at the Salon des Indépendants in 1894, is a fantastic scene with Symbolist overtones, although it depicts the horse and the piles of bodies with great precision. But the powerful vivacity of the work, with its fresh, harmonious colours, and strange lighting, is the fruit of an extraordinary imagination. The exuberance and sincerity of Rousseau's canvases astonished Pissarro and aroused his admiration. The pictorial daring, modernity and freedom of his compositions attracted the attention of Gauguin, as well as of avant-garde poets and painters such as Alfred Jarry, Guillaume Apollinaire, Robert Delaunay and Pablo Picasso, who owned several of his works, now in the Musée Picasso, Paris. The clean-cut drawing and clear shapes, bright colours and wry details that characterise Rousseau's art are to be found in the large *Portrait of a Woman* (circa 1897) with set features, viewed from the front.

But it was especially the large paintings of exotic subjects executed at the end of his life that brought Rousseau success and commissions; the dreamy exoticism of his jungles drew on magazine illustrations and frequent visits to the local zoo, the Jardin des Plantes. The flora and fauna is sometimes so daringly handled that he seems to be a forerunner of the "revolutionary" movements of the twentieth century. *The Snake Charmer* (1907) is a fine example; it was commissioned by Robert Delaunay's mother and appreciated by Apollinaire, Picasso and the Cubists. It draws the spectator into a world of mystery, dreams and imagination.

Henri Rousseau
known as Le Douanier
Rousseau
1844-1910
War
or *Discord on Horseback*
1894
Oil on canvas
114 x 105 cm
Purchased in 1946

Henri Rousseau
  known as Le Douanier
  Rousseau
  1844-1910
  The Snake Charmer
  1907

Oil on canvas
169 x 189 cm
Jacques Doucet bequest,
1936

At Pont-Aven
Paul Gauguin, Emile Bernard, Paul Sérusier

Gauguin divided his time between Brittany and the Pacific, the two main poles of attraction in his life. In 1883, Gauguin, who was an amateur painter and had been exhibiting with the Impressionists since 1880, decided "to paint every day."

In 1886, he went to Pont Aven, a picturesque town in Brittany which since 1860 had welcomed a cosmopolitan community of artists attracted by its rather archaic charm and the possibility of "living for nothing". *Washerwomen at Pont Aven* (1886), one of paintings he executed in Brittany, exhibits the vibrant, clear brushstrokes borrowed from the Impressionists' luminous style. After a trip to Martinique, with his head full of bright light and powerful colours, he returned to Pont Aven in February 1888, and wrote: "I love Brittany. There is something wild and primitive here. When my clogs strike the granite soil I hear the muffled, deadened, powerful sound I strive for in my painting." Gauguin met Emile Bernard in Pont Aven and it proved to be a decisive encounter; the dialogue and contact between these two powerful personalities was fruitful and stimulating and spurred them to develop new Cloisonnist techniques. *Earthenware Jar and Apples* bears a note by Emile Bernard on the back: "First attempt at Synthetism and simplification, 1887"; although his admiration for Cézanne is manifest, his research makes the painting a sort of sketch that highlights the process of simplification. This way of stripping away details and keeping only the essential form is also found in *Madeleine in the Bois d'Amour* (1888); Madeleine was Emile Bernard's sister, and was the "mystic muse" of Pont Aven. Here she is shown like a tomb figure beside the Aven, in the midst of a forest of column-like trees.

Haymaking in Brittany (1888) shows that Gauguin gave up Impressionism during his second stay in Pont Aven and turned to a sturdier, more strongly contrasted style. In October, under Gauguin's guidance, Paul Sérusier made a quick sketch from nature, *The Talisman* (1888) with simplified forms and flat, bright colours, and then passed the lesson on to the new group known as the Nabis.

In October 1888, Gauguin went to join Van Gogh at Arles; they painted the *Alyscamps* side by side. Gauguin created a monumental, static work, heightened with intense, flaming colours. But the episode in the south of France was short lived and ended with a dramatic separation and Gauguin's hasty return to Paris. He painted a portrait of his friend, the painter *Schuffenecker and his Family* (1889) in his studio; the high viewpoint and daring foreshortening were reminiscent of Japanese art, suggested by the print hung on the wall.

Gauguin went back to Pont Aven for the third time in 1889; he then painted his major work, *La Belle Angèle* (1889); Angèle Satre is set in a circle arranged "like a Japanese print" and her bonnet has been used for decorative purposes. For the first time, Gauguin wrote the title on the canvas. The introduction of a piece of pottery with a pre-Columbian air, functions as a second signature. *Portrait of the Artist with Yellow Christ* (1890-1891), painted a few months before he left on his first voyage to Tahiti, was bought by first Daniel de Monfreid, and then Maurice Denis, both artists, and remained long unknown to the public. Influenced by Cézanne's firm style and his way of using light to model faces, Gauguin produced a powerful image of himself as a solitary, untamed creator. *The Yellow Haystacks* (1889), a painting made up of outlined areas of solid colour, can be compared to *Harvest by the Sea* (1891) by Emile Bernard, which shows a move towards a more geometrical style under Cézanne's influence. Gauguin's last journey to Brittany, in 1894, gave rise to *Breton Women on the Road (Breton Peasant Women,* 1894),

Paul Gauguin
1848-1903
La Belle Angèle
1889
Oil on canvas
92 x 73 cm
Gift from Ambroise
Vollard, 1927

which shows the influence of Tahitian features and colouring, in a synthetic, monumental composition.

All these artists rejected the analytical approach, the "mindless imitation" of the Naturalists and Impressionists; they stripped away detail, simplified forms and used solid, simple colour.

Sérusier's work is particularly well represented in the museum's collections thanks to recent donations by Miss Henriette Boutaric. While he was in Brittany, Sérusier painted in bright flat colours, with firm dark outlines, often showing Gauguin's influence and using the same themes. His *Flowery Fence* (1889) and *Breton Wrestling* (1890-1891) are like muted echoes of Gauguin's work. *Storm* (1893) is closer to the tonalities used by his Nabi friends. Gauguin and his friends held an exhibition at the Café Volpini in 1889, which had powerful repercussions on the young Nabis. The Pont Aven period, which represents the best of the work of all these artists, was only a passing stage for Gauguin who continued his quest for things new and unknown.

Emile Bernard
1868-1941
Madeleine in the Bois d'Amour
1888
Oil on canvas
137 x 164 cm
Purchased in 1977

Paul Gauguin
1848-1903
*Portrait of the Artist
with Yellow Christ*
1890-1891
Oil on canvas
38 x 46 cm

Purchased with the
contribution of Philippe
Meyer and Japanese
sponsorship coordinated
by the newspaper
Nikkei en 1994

Paul Gauguin
1848-1903
Breton Peasant Women
1894
Oil on canvas
66 x 92.5 cm
Max and Rosy Kaganovitch
donation, 1973

The moderate success of the auction sale of his paintings, at which Degas bought *La Belle Angèle,* enabled Gauguin to set sail for Tahiti in 1891. He was fascinated by the indolent charm of the local beauties. *Tahitian Women* (1891) shows massive, tranquil bodies in a setting reduced to a few superimposed layers of dark tones; the stylisation of the red and white pareo fits in well with Gauguin's decorative scheme. *The Meal* (1891) plays on the contrast between the luxuriant, colourful fruit in the foreground and the frieze of the motionless Tahitian children: the side door suggests the bright light outside. A slightly mysterious charm emanates from *Arearea (Joyousness,* 1892), better known as *The Red Dog* because of its arbitrary colours, which fascinated the Fauves. In a masterly synthesis, he mingles the influence of Egyptian, Javanese, Japanese and Polynesian art, which he had seen at the Universal Exhibitions or during his travels. When Gauguin came back to Pont Aven for the last time in 1894, his Tahitian experience had refreshed his view of things and enriched his palette; in *Le Moulin David,* 1896, the colours are intense and more violent than in earlier works painted in Brittany.

In July 1895 he left for Tahiti again, leaving Europe for ever. His *Self-Portrait* in 1897 is dedicated to "my friend Daniel de Monfreid". Monfreid's vigilant friendship was a vital support for Gauguin, isolated on the other side of the world. The portrait matches his friend Morice's description: "A massive bony face with a narrow forehead, a nose not so much curved or hooked as broken."

In the manuscript of *Noa Noa* in which Gauguin described the gods of "a faithfully imagined Tahiti", he recounts the legend of *Vairumati,* 1897. "She was tall and the fiery sun shone in her golden flesh while all the mysteries of love slumbered in the night of her hair." All the poetry of myth lingers in this Tahitian enchantment, and Gauguin's art, like Mallarmé's poetry, lies in suggesting rather than saying. Gauguin's painting reaches back to the source of things: "I have gone right back, much further than the horses of the Parthenon, right back to the hobby horses of my childhood." (*The White Horse,* 1898)

In September 1901, he "set off for a simpler country, in search of new, more savage things," Hiva Oa, one of islands in the Marquesas group. None better than Stéphane Mallarmé has caught the essence of Gauguin's painting: "It is extraordinary to put so much mystery into such brilliance."

Paul Gauguin
1848-1903
Tahitian Women
or *On the Beach*
1891
Oil on canvas
69 x 91.5 cm
Viscount Guy de Cholet
legacy, 1923

Paul Gauguin
1848-1903
The White Horse
1898
Oil on canvas
140 x 91.5 cm
Purchased in 1927

The Nabis
Pierre Bonnard, Edouard Vuillard, Maurice Denis, Ker-Xavier Roussel

The Nabi movement can trace its origins back to October 1888, when Sérusier was painting at Pont-Aven: "How do you see this tree?" Gauguin had asked him when they were in the Bois d'Amour. "Is it green? Paint it green then, the most beautiful green on your palette; - and this shadow, rather blue? Go ahead and paint it as blue as you can."

The dazzling landscape painted by Sérusier under Gauguin's guidance and called *The Talisman* (1888) was a revelation for his friends at the Julian Académie, Paul Ranson, Denis and Bonnard who in turn inspired other admirers, Edouard Vuillard and Ker-Xavier Roussel. *The Talisman,* which prompted Maurice Denis to paint two "patchy" paintings, shows the significance of Gauguin's lesson; each of these works was "so synthetically designed as to become a 'shapeless landscape', almost abstract, a hymn to the juxtaposition of pure colour. *On the Road to Calvary* (1889), Maurice Denis' earliest religious painting, and even more forcefully *Patches of Sun on the Terrace* (1890) are dazzling demonstrations that art is, in its own terms, a 'transposition', "the passionate equivalent of a sensation."

These young artists banded together in a sort of confraternity and called themselves the "nabis" (the Hebrew word for prophets), some with a touch of irony and others out of conviction. They were bonded by their friendship and their shared aspiration to create a new art form, and they formed the avant-garde in Paris in the closing decade of the nineteenth century. As prophets of a new form of art, they chose to ignore the traditional rules of painting and turned to "medieval stained glass windows, Japanese prints and Egyptian painting," in the words of the group's theorist, Denis.

Starting from these few shared ideas, each artist developed his own style; Bonnard, fairly named the 'Japanese Nabi', chose a long narrow canvas like a screen, tender humour and an intimate atmosphere for *Child with a Bucket,* which

Paul Sérusier
1863-1927
The Talisman
1888
Oil on wood
27 x 22 cm
Purchased with the
contribution of
Mr Philippe Meyer
through the Lutèce
Foundation, 1985

Pierre Bonnard
1867-1947
The Checked Bodice
1892
Oil on canvas
61 x 33 cm
Purchased in 1968

Maurice Denis
1870-1943
Calvary
or *Calvary Hill*
1889

Oil on canvas
41 x 32.5 cm
Gift from Dominique
Maurice Denis, 1986

depicts one of his nephews wearing a kimono, with the nape of his neck bared, playing in Bonnard's family property in Dauphiné. The same garden was a setting for *Twilight (Game of Croquet,* 1892) which shows members of his family like so many decorative cut-out silhouettes filling a space with several perspectives. Several years later, *The Big Garden* (1894) used the same setting, but in a symphony of paler greens.

Bonnard's four panels of *Women in the Garden (1891)* made up his first decorative ensemble, which was exhibited at the seventh Salon des Indépendants. The curving lines of the drawing in an Art Nouveau spirit, the long narrow canvas, and the plant motifs cutting across the compositions are all pointers to the artist's interest in Japanese art. He admitted drawing on Japanese prints for his checked patterns (*Checked Bodice,* 1892); after 1894, he seems to have been more strongly attracted by interiors and domestic scenes in which he used artificial lighting (*Under the Lamp,* 1899). *Intimacy* (1891) gives a free, familiar glimpse of the composer Claude Terrasse (1867-1923), who is enjoying a smoke and a chat in an astonishing composition which introduces two other characters, one standing at the side, against the light, and the other invisible except for a hand and a pipe in a swirl of smoke in the foreground.

The Indolent Woman (1899) is one of his first nudes, a theme which later became a favourite. Bonnard has painted her in darker colours. The bird's-eye view tips the space until it fills the entire canvas; it was at this period that Bonnard and Vuillard were aesthetically most in harmony.

At the beginning of his career, Edouard Vuillard was perhaps the most fervent Nabi of all; *In Bed* (1891) provides ample proof of that. This familiar, intimate sub-

Pierre Bonnard
1867-1947
Woman Lying on a Bed
or *The Indolent Woman*
1899
Oil on canvas
96 x 106 cm
Purchased in 1947

Pierre Bonnard
1867-1947
Twilight
or *Game of Croquet*
1892
Oil on canvas
130 x 162 cm

Gift from Daniel
Wildenstein through
the Friends of the Musée
d'Orsay, 1985

The Nabis
Pierre Bonnard, Edouard Vuillard, Maurice Denis, Ker-Xavier Roussel

Pierre Bonnard
1867-1947
Child with a Sand Castle
Distemper on canvas
162 x 50 cm
Purchased with the help
of *Yomiuri Shimbun*, 1982

Pierre Bonnard
1867-1947
*Woman with a Checked
Dress*
1891
Distemper on paper glued
on canvas
160 x 48 cm
Accepted in lieu
of inheritance tax, 1984

Pierre Bonnard
1867-1947
Woman in a Cloak
1891
Distemper on paper glued
on canvas
160 x 48 cm
Accepted in lieu
of inheritance tax, 1984

ject is arranged in an astonishing way; the areas of flat, superimposed colour use a narrow range of beiges. The long slumping line of the body suggests sleep and the arbitrary distortion of the human figure produces a very daring form of stylisation.

About 1890, the Nabis demanded "walls to decorate" to embellish the everyday environment, which was also an overriding concern in all Art Nouveau. *Still Life with a Lettuce*, with its subtle, pearly tones, was very probably part of a set painted by Vuillard in 1887-1888 to decorate his dining room. But his talents as a decorator emerged most strongly in *Public Gardens* (1894). The museum has five of the nine panels, presented in a corner as they were in the house of the man who commissioned them, Alexandre Natanson. (Other panels are in museums in Brussels, Cleveland and Houston.) Natanson, who was the director of the *Revue Blanche*, actively supported these young avant-garde artists, publishing their engravings and exhibiting their work. The arbitrary cropping of these five compositions, influenced by Japanese art, enhances the astonishing foreshortening; the use of distemper gives extra substance and it is laid on in large simplified areas intended to be seen from a distance. The slightly asymmetrical rhythm of the panels interacts with the movement of the figures, while the delicate colour harmonies and subtle tones vibrate in a minor mode; the overall effect is grave and serenely charming.

Vuillard's originality can be seen, too, in a number of small whimsical panels in a caricatural vein (*Woman in a Green Hat, Side View*, 1891) in which the figure is outlined against a neutral background, with large areas of colour and the same taste for synthesis as is found in *Sleep* (1891).

The Swiss painter Félix Vallotton moved to Paris in 1882; the ingenious, humorous arrangement of *The Ball* (1899) makes good use of the concise style and large areas of flat colour which were characteristic of Nabi aesthetics. The realism and

Edouard Vuillard
1868-1940
Woman with a Green Hat
Circa 1891
Oil on cardboard
21 x 16 cm
Accepted in lieu
of inheritance tax, 1990

Félix Vallotton
1865-1925
The Ball
1899
Paint diluted with
turpentine and gouache
on cardboard

49.5 x 61.9 cm
Carle Dreyfus bequest,
1953

Edouard Vuillard
1868-1940
In Bed
1891
Oil on canvas

74 x 92 cm
Oral bequest by the artist,
executed by Mr and
Mrs Ker-Xavier Roussel,
1941

Edouard Vuillard
1868-1940
Decorative panels for
Alexandre Natanson's
dining room
(Public Gardens)
Distemper on canvas
1864

Little Girls Playing
215 x 88 cm
Mrs Alexandre Radot
bequest, 1978

The Interrogation
215 x 92 cm
Mrs Alexandre Radot
bequest, 1978

The Nursemaids
213 x 73 cm
Purchased in 1929

meticulous execution of *Dinner, Lamplight* (1899) captures the artist's family in a slightly caricatured manner, under a striking light in glossy, contrasting colours; Vallotton was a forerunner of the Expressionists in his use of sharp lines and even prefigured some Surrealist effects. He handled landscapes with subtlety; *Moonlight* (circa 1895), with its flowing lines, Symbolist overtones and silent, mysterious mood, is unusual for Vallotton because he did not fully develop this genre until 1910-1911.

Aristide Maillol started out as a painter and joined the Nabi group, whose ideas he shared: the decorative style of the precise profile of *Woman with a Sunshade* (circa 1895) stands out against a simplified background similar to the tapestries

Conversation
213 x 154 cm
Purchased in 1929

The Red Parasol
214 x 81 cm
Purchased in 1929

The Nabis
Pierre Bonnard, Edouard Vuillard, Maurice Denis, Ker-Xavier Roussel

he was working on at the time. The subject matter and the colours bring him close to the Impressionists.

Maurice Denis was the theorist of the group; his famous definition: a painting "is essentially a flat surface covered with colours arranged in a certain order" could apply to any Nabi work, especially his early canvases and also to *The Muses* (1893). Denis' deep, matt palette lent itself to bold simplification and accentuated the decorative nature of the painting. The stylisation of form and the use of arabesques in the rendering of foliage, created an unreal poetic atmosphere, similar to the Symbolists' work. *The Muses* is a sort of remake of Puvis de Chavannes' *Sacred Wood.* 1893 was a year of achievement; a procession of girls is walking under *The Green Trees (Landscape with Green Trees* or *The Beeches of Kerduel,* 1893) of which only the trunks can be seen; one of the girls is going to meet an angel. A silent, symbolic place, on the fringe between the natural and supernatural worlds, *Landscape with Green Trees* illustrates one of the artist's favourite themes, infused with poetry and mysticism.

The admiration that Denis and other members of the group felt for Cézanne, Gauguin and Odilon Redon, whom they regarded as their 'initiators', found an outlet in *Homage to Cézanne* (1900). Like Fantin-Latour's *Homages,* Denis grouped the main Nabis around a still life by Cézanne which had belonged to Gauguin (from left to right: Redon, Vuillard, André Mellerio, Ambroise Vollard, Denis, Sérusier, Ranson, Roussel, Bonnard and Marthe Denis). The scene is set in the Vollard gallery in the presence of their elder, Redon, and the art critc Mellerio; this work is a useful document because it is a set of portraits of all the Nabis and shows that the group was still united as late as 1900.

At the turn of the century, a change was perceptible in the work of most of the Nabis. They moved away from the flat colour of their youth, abandoned simplification and softened their colours.

Denis was one of the first to understand Cézanne, well before the great retrospective of the Salon d'Automne in 1907, which made him the acknowledged master of the young generation. Denis had been a regular visitor to the Louvre since his childhood and his first visit to Fiesole, in 1895, had sparked a passion for the Italian primitives, especially Fra Angelico; a second stay in Italy, in Florence and Rome in 1897-1897, and his encounter with André Gide, strengthened his desire to blend the individual in a universal harmony. Thus when he painted simple, happy scenes, such as *Breton Women under the Trellis,* an evocation that cannot be dissociated from its pictorial history, or *Paradise* (1912), a picture of the flower garden in his house Silencio, which he bought at Perros-Guirec in 1908, he also suggested a golden age open to all.

Maurice Denis
1870-1943
The Muses
1893
Oil on canvas
168 x 135 cm
Purchased in 1932

Maurice Denis
1870-1943
Landscape with Green Trees or
Beeches at Kerduel or *The Green Trees*
1893
Oil on canvas
46 x 43 cm
Accepted in lieu of inheritance tax,
2001

Félix Vallotton
1865-1925
Moonlight
Circa 1895
Oil on canvas
27 x 41 cm
Purchased in 1979

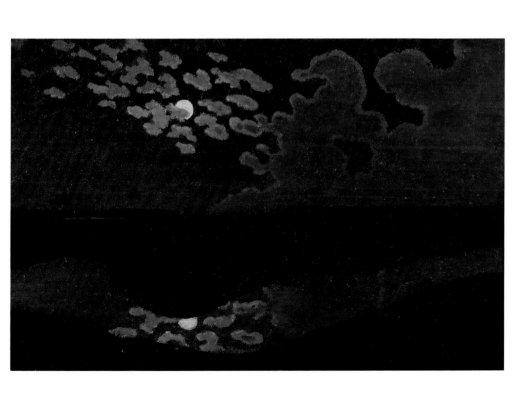

Reproduced in dictionaries and school textbooks then completely forgotten after the 1920-1930s, a number of paintings that were famous and even popular at the time typified the official taste of the Third Republic. Despite a wide range of subject matter, they all illustrate the naturalist trends which developed in France in the 1880-1890s.

Jules Bastien-Lepage, who painted peasant life and work in the fields, was receptive to the modern mood; his painting is clear with a fairly free style inspired by Manet and his friends. *Haymaking* makes him one of the best examples of official naturalist painting, which is also represented by Alfred Roll, who was skilled in rendering fresh, healthy, sweeping country scenes (*Manda Lamétrie, Farmer's Wife*, 1887). Lhermite's peasants, resolute and valiant, introduce a social resonance in his portrayal of the agricultural world and *Payday for the Harvesters*, which was bought by the state, confirmed his reputation.

Fernand Cormon dealt with another aspect of modern life in *The Forge* (1894), a painting in subdued colours with brief gleams of light; however, Cormon specialised in prehistoric scenes and religious history. For his *Cain*, the key work in the Salon of 1880, which illustrates a poem by Victor Hugo taken from *La Légende des Siècles*, Cormon worked from a model for each figure, showing a concern for archaeological realism in his evocation of primitive life. The painting was generally well received and was bought from Cormon by the State.

Jean-Paul Laurens focused on dramatic episodes from French history, here *The Excommunication of Robert the Pious* (1875). Léon Bonnat started as a history painter and later concentrated on portraiture, painting the official portraits of all the personalities of the Third Republic; the personality of the majestic actress *Madame Pasca* is conveyed by the veracity of her presence, heightened by the

Jean-Paul Laurens
1838-1921
*The Excommunication
of Robert the Pious*
1875
Oil on canvas
130 x 218 cm
Purchased by the state
from the artist, 1875

Léon Bonnat
1833-1922
Portrait of Madame Pasca
1874
Oil on canvas
222.5 x 132 cm
Arthur Pernolet legacy,
1915

Edouard Detaille
1848-1912
The Dream
1888
Oil on canvas
300 x 400 cm
Purchased in 1888

Jules Bastien-Lepage
1848-1884
Haymaking
Oil on canvas
180 x 195 cm
Purchased in 1885

Fernand-Anne Piestre
known as **Cormon**
1845-1924
Cain
1880
Oil on canvas
584 x 700 cm
Purchased in 1880

"When, with his children, dressed in animal skins,
his hair tousled and livid in the midst of the storm,
Cain fled before Jehovah, just as night was falling,
the grim man came to the foot of a mountain in a vast plain..."

Victor Hugo, *La Légende des siècles*, 1859

colours and lighting. The naturalist movement spread from France to the whole of Europe; Marie Bashkirtseff, who came to work in Paris, was strongly influenced by her master Bastien-Lepage *(The Meeting,* 1884).

The ardent, melancholic region of Brittany became a favourite haunt for a group of artists known as the "black gang", who were strongly affected by the violent contrasts in the region. Charles Cottet and Lucien Simon depicted the rough life of seafaring men using dark colours in a realistic manner derived from Courbet. Cottet's shadowy painting with its arrested gestures, and pained and resigned figures, expresses a heavy sense of fatality (*In the Land of the Sea,* 1898; *Grief in the Land of the Sea,* 1908).

Max Liebermann
1874-1935
Country Bar at Brannenburg
1893
Oil on canvas
70 x 100 cm
Purchased by the state from the artist, 1894

Charles Cottet
1863-1925
Grief in a Seafaring Country
1908
Oil on canvas
264 x 345 cm
Purchased in 1912

The naturalist movement spread across Europe. The German artist Max Liebermann, whose work shows affinities with Impressionism, used luminous touches to catch the sun filtering through leaves (*Country Bar at Brannenburg*, 1893). The same influence is found in the refined intimist portrait of *Mme Lwoff* (1895) by the Russian painter Valentin Serov, in which the light sets up colourful vibrations on her face and pale bodice.

The same exploration of the light was going on in Scandinavia: the Danish painter Peder Krøyer introduced the taste for open air painting and light to Denmark. He captured the vivacity, freshness and clarity of the sea air at Skagen (*Fishing Boats*, 1884). An authentic, natural light also dwells in the powerful, warm painting of the Spaniard Sorolla y Batida (*Return of the Fishing Boats*; *Hauling the Boat*).

The Dutch painter Hendrik Breitner prolonged the Realist tradition; influenced by Courbet, Millet, Manet and Naturalist literature (Zola), he sought to be a witness of his times. Settled in Amsterdam in 1886, Breitner became the portraitist of the city, painting scenes of everyday life in broad strokes and dark colours; his *Horses Hauling Logs in Amsterdam* conveys the horses' ponderous strength. *Moonlight* (circa 1887-1889) is an exceptionally stripped back work, in which enormous clouds roll across a vast sky above the deserted countryside.

In Switzerland, Eugène Brunand painted in a naturalist style for his religious works. *The Disciples Peter and John Running to the Tomb* (1898), one of his most famous works, reveals his grasp of dramatic effects in the composition, lighting and facial expressions.

Lastly, the Belgian artist Léon Frédéric, in his carefully crafted, almost hyper-realist triptych *The Ages of the Worker* (1895-1897), painted in cold colours, explores the same social symbolism as Eugène Laermans (*Late Autumn*, 1899).

Valentin Alexandrovitch Serov
1864-1955
Mrs Lwoff, the artist's cousin
1895
Oil on canvas
90 x 59 cm
Donation by
Professor André Lwoff
and Mr Stéphane Lwoff,
the model's sons, 1980

Georg-Hendrik Breitner
1857-1923
Two White Horses
Hauling Logs in
Amsterdam
Circa 1897-1898

Oil on canvas
100 x 152 cm
Purchased in 1982

Eugène Burnand
1850-1921
The Disciples Peter
and John Running to
the Tomb on the Morning
of the Resurrection
1898

Oil on canvas
82 x 134 cm
Purchased in 1898

Naturalism In Paris
Jacques-Emile Blanche, Giovanni Boldini

The brilliant, elegant, cosmopolitan crowd that haunted the theatres, cafés and salons of Paris soon became a favourite subject for painters and sculptors and its light, witty atmosphere invaded literature, as illustrated by Marcel Proust (1871-1922). It was in 1891 that Jacques-Emile Blanche met the writer, of whom he has left this famous portrait, showing his face against a dark background that heightens the pale accents of Proust's shirt and the orchid. One of the best-known figures in Paris at the time was Count Robert de Montesquiou, an aesthete, Symbolist writer and man of the world. It was in Montesquiou's circle that Proust found the models for the main characters in *Remembrance of Time Past*, Montesquiou himself inspiring the character of Baron Charlus. Boldini moved to Paris in 1872 and began his famous series of Parisian portraits *(Robert de Montesquiou)*, society women or women of the demi-monde like *Madame Max* (1896). Sarah Bernhardt, who then reigned over the stage, was one of the muses of this Parisian set.

The Salon, which dominated artistic, cultural and social affairs at the end of the century, put its stamp of approval on official taste and a system of selection illustrated by Henri Gervex's painting, *A Painting Jury* (1885). Laurens, Léon Bonnat, Alexandre Cabanel and Jules Lefebvre can be recognised among the members of the jury, as well as more independent personalities such as Puvis de Chavannes or Cormon. The artists maintained the distinction between genres and the primacy of history, mythology and allegory, which were pretexts for the female nudes so appreciated by art collectors. This was the case for William Bouguereau (*The Birth of Venus*, 1879) whose ideal was purely decorative.

André Devambez gave a more disturbing view of Paris life. Painted with the verve and dynamism of a journalist taking a snapshot, *The Charge* (1902) recalled that the Belle Epoque was also a time of social unrest before the great hecatomb.

André Devambez
1867-1944
The Charge
1902
Oil on canvas
127 x 162 cm
Purchased in 1979

Jacques-Emile Blanche
1861-1942
Portrait of Marcel Proust
1892
73.5 x 60.5 cm
Accepted in lieu
of inheritance tax, 1989

Giovanni Boldini
1842-1931
Madame Max
1896
Oil on canvas
205 x 100 cm
Gift from Mrs Charles
Max, 1904

France was one of the most active centres of the international Symbolist movement, which developed in reaction to Realism and Impressionism. Refusing a world dominated by science and machines, intellectuals and artists tried to translate the untranslatable, that is, thought, reveries and dreams. That explains the many variations within the movement both in their themes and their means of expression.

"I do not believe what I touch or what I see. I believe only what I do not see and only what I feel." A late convert to Romanticism, inspired by Delacroix and Chassériau, attracted by anything strange and precious, Gustave Moreau made his mark at the Salon of 1865 with *Jason and Medea* and even more forcefully at the Salon of 1866 with the very famous *Thracian Girl Carrying the Head of Orpheus,* which was immediately purchased by the state. These paintings bring out the languid grace of Moreau's heroes and the refined richness of his colours, as well as his gifts as a miniaturist painter and the strange accessories he used; thus the column that figures in *Jason* is encrusted with pearls and cameos and colourful hummingbirds add a bright note to the background.

The Orpheus myth, which proved to be a favourite Symbolist theme since it showed that the artist lives on through his creations or his ideas, is given one of its first and most original interpretations here. A woman covered with jewels, colourful, iridescent, hieratic and often perverse, has the foremost role in Moreau's oeuvre. *Galatea,* a fragile girl in a cave, is faced with the monstrous figure and brute strength of the Cyclops.

Moreau's free approach to his teaching at the Ecole des Beaux-Arts attracted the young Fauves, such as Matisse and Marquet, and independent artists such as Georges Rouault, who was one of his most loyal pupils. In 1898, he bequeathed his studio at 14 rue de La Rouchefoucauld, with all the works it contained, to the state. Now a museum, with the works hung as Moreau wished, it contains thousands of works of all sizes and using all techniques and lends some on a rotational basis to the Musée d'Orsay.

At the other end of the spectrum from Gustave Moreau, Eugène Carrière painted scenes from family life and childhood in a narrow range of browns; a misty effect gives this familiar world an unreal feeling. The portrait of *Paul Verlaine* pays homage to the poet who was a precursor of, and with Mallarmé, an intellectual guide for the Symbolist poets.

Gustave Moreau
1826-1898
Galatea
1880
Oil on wood
85.5 x 66 cm
Purchased with the help
of Philippe Meyer,
Japanese sponsorship
coordinated by
the newspaper *Nikkei* and
a contribution from the
Heritage Fund, 1997

Gustave Moreau
1826-1898
Orpheus
1866
Oil on wood
154 x 99.5 cm
Purchased in 1866

From the time it was painted in 1881, *The Poor Fisherman* fascinated all who saw it. Critics, poets and men of letters, even if they did not share the same views, could not resist writing about it, highlighting its Symbolism or its classicism. But above all, the work attracted the attention of artists such as Gauguin, Seurat, Signac, Redon, Carrière, Maillol, Maurice Denis and even Picasso. The restrained emotion that emanates from the painting is obtained by the dominant voids, subdued colours, lack of movement, shadows and modelling and a timeless landscape. The same sense of monumentality and sparing composition is found in *Girls by the Sea* (1879), whose modulated colours and calm lines suggest an atmosphere of peace and melancholic inner joy, leaving wide scope for Symbolist interpretations. Even in a familiar theme such as *Woman at her Toilette* (1883), Puvis de Chavannes leaves an impression of dreamy eternity. His easel paintings use the same pale, matt paint as his large decorative murals (museums in Amiens, Marseilles, Lyons and Rouen; town halls in Poitiers, Paris; the Sorbonne, the Panthéon).

The Balloon (1870) and *The Pigeon* (1871), both in a range of browns, with large female figures in mourning, are a moving symbol of the resistance of the Parisians. Indeed, it was when he was keeping watch on the ramparts during the Siege of Paris that Puvis had the idea for *The Ball;* he added a companion piece, showing a homing pigeon escaping a hawk soaring above a snow-covered Ile de la Cité.

Summer (1873), one of his favourite themes, is impregnated with a calm, poetic atmosphere and the monumental, decorative breadth that is characteristic of his work.

Pierre Puvis de Chavannes
1824-1898
The Balloon
1870
Oil on canvas
136.7 x 86.5 cm
Gift of Gallery Acquavella,
New York, 1987

The Pigeon
1871
Oil on canvas
136.7 x 86.5 cm
Gift of Gallery Acquavella,
New York, 1987

Pierre Puvis de Chavannes
1824-1898
The Poor Fisherman
Salon of 1881
Oil on canvas
155 x 192.5 cm
Purchased in 1887

Pierre Puvis de Chavannes
1824-1898
Girls by the Sea
Salon of 1879
Oil on canvas
205 x 154 cm
Gift from Robert Gérard,
1970

Odilon Redon

A close friend of the poet Stéphane Mallarmé, the "prince of mysterious dreams", Redon delighted in dreams and the invisible world. He first explored drawing and lithography, and turned to colour in 1890 with *Closed Eyes* (1890), which he himself felt was "a trifle grey". The painting seems to illustrate one of Redon's remarks: "In art, everything happens through docile submission to the unconscious." This impressive face, with the closed eyelids conducive to thought, imitates the posture of Michelangelo's *Dying Slaves,* which Redon had admired in the Louvre. The smudged brushstrokes give a vaporous, impalpable effect, which strengthens the deep inwardness and spirituality of this astonishing vision, proclaiming the triumph of mind over matter, and dream over reason. Redon kept his original style even in his portraits. *The Black Profile* (1903-1905), a posthumous portrait of his friend Gauguin, is a poetic, moving image of the artist's singular head surrounded by a halo of strange flowers.

The off-centre, pensive, restrained *Portrait of Baroness Robert de Domecy* (1900) seems to be set against a background of flowers and light. Robert de Domecy was a faithful admirer of Redon's work and in 1899 asked him to decorate the dining room of his château, which was nearing completion at the time. It was the first time Redon had tackled such a project and he was anxious, but created a set of fifteen panels peopled, he wrote, "with dream flowers, and imaginary animals; all on big panels using a bit of everything, distemper, lanoline, oils and even pastels...". The panels were finished in October 1901 and were hung above dark oak woodwork, while friezes around the windows and above the doors lit up the room with their flaming yellow and blue. This decoration marked Redon's dazzling entry into the world of colour for he never returned to black and white. It was also a prelude to many other decorative works and strengthened the artist's desire to participate in the ideas of the Art Nouveau movement – embellishing everyday sur-

Odilon Redon
1840-1916
*Portrait of Baroness
Robert de Domecy*
1900
Oil on canvas
74.3 x 68.5 cm
Purchased in 1994 by
the Société des amis
du Musée d'Orsay,
with the participation
of Philippe Meyer

Odilon Redon
1840-1916
Closed Eyes
1890
Oil on cardboard
44 x 36 cm
Purchased in 1904

roundings and taking the same care over a decorative work as over an easel painting. In 1904, he tackled the theme of the female nude (*Eve*), giving her a supple, powerful image, a blend of gravity and mystery that he regarded as an integral part of womanly grace and seduction.

Brightly coloured pastel was the best medium for his ambivalent, fantastic visions (*Buddha*, 1905). In counterpoint to this work, which gave Symbolism its richest pictorial expression, he painted admirable *Bouquets of Flowers,* and, for his own pleasure, small landscapes in Brittany or in his native Bordeaux region - simple, well-observed realistic sketches. Thanks to the generosity of Suzanne and Ari Redon, the artist's son, the Musée d'Orsay has a large collection of pastels and landscapes. The Claude Roger-Marx donation enables the museum to rotate other graphic works by Redon, Bresdin, Bonnard and Daumier.

Quite a different vision, in a more traditional manner, was given by Alphonse Osbert, who painted forests and lakes peopled by timeless female figures, in flowing white clothing, or by Lucien Lévy-Dhurmer, with his strange, sometimes vehement pastels (*Medusa* or *The Furious Wave,* 1897);

Odilon Redon
1840-1916
Tree against a Yellow Background
Decorative panel for the dining room of the Château de Domecy
1901
Oil on canvas
249 x 185 cm
Accepted in lieu of inheritance tax, 1988

Odilon Redon
1840-1916
Portrait of Gauguin
Painted between 1903
and 1905
Oil on canvas
66 x 54.5 cm
Purchased in 1950

Odilon Redon
1840-1916
The Buddha
Circa 1905
Pastel on beige paper
90 x 73 cm
Purchased in 1971

Symbolism outside France

One of the first Symbolist movements appeared in Great Britain; the Pre-Raphaelite group was formed in 1848 in opposition to contemporary trends, proclaimed its rejection of reality and its desire to explore Gothic art and fifteenth-century Italian painting and everything before Raphael. Edward Burne-Jones, a fervent admirer of Botticelli and Michelangelo, transformed a traditional subject *The Wheel of Fortune* (1883) into a monumental work whose pensive figures, beautiful in an idealistic, nostalgic way, were noticed and admired by Puvis de Chavannes and his contemporaries.

The landscape was also a popular theme with the Symbolists; tinged with lyricism and romanticism in the work of the Swiss painter Arnold Böcklin (*Diana Hunting*, circa 1896), or bucolic in Ménard's huge canvases. Ménard reconstituted a mythical Greek world in which the colonnades of temples and pine trees fade into twilight and silence (*The Golden Age*, a decoration for the Paris law school). The German Hans Thoma was close to Böcklin, but did not use mythological themes; instead he explored inhabited landscapes derived from Poussin (*Siesta*, 1889).

In Italy, Pellizza da Volpedo, who was interested in Seurat's research, used the Divisionist technique to capture the play of light and express the mysteries of life and death (*Crushed Flower*, circa 1896-1902).

Belgian Symbolism, an important, lively movement, varied with the temperament of each artist. Fernand Khnopff, regarded as the leader of the Belgian Symbolist school, gave a vision of a silent, melancholy world with his portrait of *Marie Monnom* (wife of the painter Théo Van Rysselberghe, 1887). Far removed from this simplicity, the middle-class bedroom of *Lady in Distress* by James Ensor is a place of anguish: furniture, curtains and carpets in dull colours create a disturbing,

Sir Edward Burne-Jones
1833-1898
The Wheel of Fortune
1883
Oil on canvas
200 x 100 cm
Purchased in 1980

Fernand Khnopff
1858-1921
Marie Monnom, daughter
of the Brussels publisher,
(later Mrs Théo Van
Rysselberghe)
1887

Oil on canvas
49.5 x 50 cm
Purchased in 1981

Giuseppe Pellizza
da Volpedo
1868-1907
Crushed Flower
1896-1902
Oil on canvas
79.5 x 107 cm
Purchased in 1910

oppressive atmosphere. Jean Delville, with *Plato's School* (1898), practiced an excessive form of idealistic, intellectual Symbolism, well served by precise drawing and the sumptuous cold colours which are typical of his work.

A large pastel by Jan Toorop, almost in monochrome with occasional white heightening, staged *Desire* and *Appeasement* (1893), two monumental, hieratic, stylised figures in a mysterious setting. His studied, graphic style is close to that of the Vienna Sezession; Toorop gave this project for a stained glass window to Maurice Denis in 1911. Karel Masek adopted Seurat's Divisionist technique in 1893-1894 but his style also suggests Byzantine mosaics. *The Prophetess Libuse* (1893), queen of Bohemia in the early eighth century, is shown in a prophetic trance, holding a branch from the Slavs' sacred linden tree in her hand. The atmosphere is supernatural and decadent.

Silence and mystery reign in the interiors painted by the Dane Vilhem Hammershøi; they are empty or peopled by a lone female figure usually seen from the back, offering a "reverie on the strangeness of ordinary things". *Rest* (1905) shows his sparing, subtle technique, the thin paint and light touch and an almost monochrome palette using shades of grey, black and white, heightened with deep red.

The American Winslow Homer, a native of Boston, conjured up the mysterious world of the sea and its links with human destiny in *Summer Night* (1890). This bewitching, poetic canvas, unique in Homer's work, painted in a narrow range of blue, blue-green, slate grey, and greyish brown, and enlivened by sharp touches of white and yellow, expresses the sweetness and illusion of life faced with the secrets and power of the elements, the unknown world of the night and the sea.

Jan Toorop
1858-1928
Desire and Satisfaction
or *Appeasement*
1893
Pastel on beige paper
glued on cardboard
76 x 90 cm
Purchased in 1976

Vilhelm Hammershøï
1864-1916
Hvile (Rest)
1905
Oil on canvas
49.5 x 46.5 cm
Purchased with the
participation of Philippe
Meyer in June 1996

Winslow Homer
1836-1910
Summer Night
1890
Oil on canvas
76.7 x 102 cm
Purchased in 1900

Whereas the Universal Exhibition of 1900 had established the reputation of the Impressionists and the Symbolists, the Nabis disbanded in 1903 when the Natanson brothers ceased publication of *La Revue Blanche*. Although the members of the group remained fast friends, they went their separate ways as artists. However, in 1905, when the Salon d'Automne opened, the organisers significantly gave pride of place to Bonnard, Vuillard, Roussel and Vallotton and their initial membership of the Nabi group left a lasting imprint on their work.

Small exhibitions put on by the Bernheim brothers, who were art dealers, brought Vuillard into the public eye in 1900. In 1904, Camille Mauclair talked of him as "an intimist painter of rare delicacy, one of the people whose modesty we regret... in the presence of remarkable gifts." The apparently descriptive *Chapel of the Château de Versailles* (1917-1919, reworked in 1926-1928) reveals his virtuosity. Within the rigorous, austere architectural frame, we glimpse the mane of hair of a person seen from the back. *The Library*, a large decorative panel that Vuillard painted in 1911 for Princess Bassiano, demonstrates his ability to create a "warm, peaceful unity" with great decorative inventiveness and muted but intense colours. Among the society portraits, that of *Madame de Polignac* (1930) shows Vuillard's skill in handling space and the play of light. The model for the dome of the Champs-Elysées theatre shows how Denis used symbols to stir feelings, in a logical approach which leaves the spectator as little thinking to do as possible. His four panels evoke dance, opera, symphony and lyric drama. Dubbed the "Nabi of the beautiful icons", Maurice Denis painted many decorative works on religious themes in the second part of his life.

Roussel often used mythological themes, especially for decorative work. *The Rape of the Daughters of Leucippus* (1911) illustrates how neatly he fitted this mythological story into a real landscape.

A Bourgeois Afternoon (1900) was a pivotal work in Bonnard's career, marking the point at which he abandoned the Japanese influences and Art Nouveau of his earlier works; the decorative layout and the comic distortion are still there, but this

Maurice Denis
1870-1943
*Model for the ceiling
of the Champs Elysées Theatre*
1911
Distemper on reinforced
plaster
Diam. 240 cm

Edouard Vuillard
1868-1910
The Chapel of the
Château of Versailles
1917-1919
Oil on canvas
96 x 66 cm

Donation by Jacques
Laroche with a life
interest, 1947;
entered the museum in
1976

Edouard Vuillard
1868-1940
The Library
1911
Oil on canvas
400 x 300 cm
Purchased in 1935

large canvas, with its fixed, strange mood, is new for Bonnard. *The Woman with a Cat* (1912) brings together three of his favourite subjects: his companion Martha, the cat and a set table. But instead of the dark colours of his early work, he has used pale colours creating back-lighting that plunges Martha into soft shadow. In this painting, the link with the Nabi period can be seen in the liberty he takes with perspective, strongly influenced by Japanese art. He gains perfect mastery of the rhythm of the composition by opposing curves (the face, table, plates and shoulders) to straight lines (the fireplaces, wall and chair) and using the cat as a link between them.

"All my life," Bonnard told George Besson, "I have floated between intimist painting and decoration." *In the Boat* (1907) perfectly illustrates this ambivalence in opposing the intimacy of the scene in the foreground with the very accomplished decorative effect of the background. When he started painting, Bonnard, like most of his contemporaries, distrusted Impressionism, but here we can sense its influence and measure the distance he has travelled. For Bonnard did not paint in the open air and did not try to catch the movement of light, preferring to dominate his subject. And his perception of space and his flamboyant, iridescent colours justify André Lhote's remark that his works "bring out the purest values of painting at the expense of immediate reality." In 1906, Misia Sert commissioned Bonnard to paint a set of four decorative canvases, executed between 1906 and 1910, *Pleasure, Landscape with Bathers, After the Downpour* and *Fountains,* which the Musée d'Orsay was able to purchase in 1996. The set takes us on a journey into

Ker-Xavier Roussel
1867-1944
The Rape of the Daughters of Leucippus
Oil on canvas
273 x 165 cm
Purchased in 1935

Pierre Bonnard
1867-1947
Boating
Circa 1907
Oil on canvas
278 x 301 cm
Purchased in 1946

vaguely defined places, where contemporary figures gaze at scenes of mythical Antiquity and oriental enchantment, in a humorous, poetic, offbeat way typical of Bonnard. The painting is surrounded by an irregular orange border alive with monkeys and magpies, a sort of prelude to a fairytale opera, evoking the exotic tapestries of the eighteenth century and Puvis de Chavannes' decorative works with their foliage borders. Bonnard's first exhibition with Josse and Gaston Bernheim dates from 1906; *The Lodge* (1908) shows the two brothers, who were close friends of Bonnard's, with their wives. This theme, already explored by Renoir, Cassatt and Toulouse-Lautrec, was very freely handled; the main figure is only partly visible, for his face is cut off at eye level. The vivid colours do not manage to dispel the atmosphere of "distinguished boredom" that emanates from this painting. *The Bernheim de Villers Brothers* (1920) are also shown in their gallery in the boulevard de la Madeleine; it is an innovative work in its dazzling lighting, bold layout, and binary composition (two doors, two paintings, two figures, two light sources), and draws its rhythm from the lines and right angles which break the diagonal lines of the two dark, hieratic figures.

In 1931, Bonnard painted a painful, almost tragic image of himself as *The Boxer.* He is back-lit, standing bare-chested in front of a mirror, with clenched fists raised.

The joy in colour was taken still further by the Fauves. The movement is eloquently represented in the Musée d'Orsay thanks to the donation in 1973 of the collection that belonged to the art dealers and discerning collectors Max and Rosy Kagonovitch. André Derain and Maurice Vlaminck were close friends and revelled in pure, flamboyant colour; yellows, greens, blues and pinks violently light up

Pierre Bonnard
1867-1947
Fountains or *The Journey*
1906-1910
Oil on canvas
230 x 300 cm
Purchased with the
Heritage Fund, 1996

Pierre Bonnard
1867-1947
The Lodge
1908
Oil on canvas
91 x 120 cm
Accepted in lieu
of inheritance tax, 1989

Pierre Bonnard
*Portrait of the Bernheim
Brothers*
1920
Oil on canvas

165.5 x 155.5 cm
Gift from Mr and
Mrs Gaston Bernheim
de Villers, 1951

London's *Charing Cross Bridge*; the curve of the bridge gives powerful dynamism to all the elements in one of Fauvism's most successful paintings.

At the turn of the century, Gustav Klimt, Edvard Munch and Ferdinand Hodler, closely associated with Symbolism and attracted to landscape, heralded the arrival of new trends. The Austrian Klimt was one of the founder members of the Vienna Sezession who rebelled against the recognised academic organisations and historicism; his constantly evolving style went from dark, sentimental landscapes to the representation of nature perceived as a protective tissue. *Roses under the Trees*, a mosaic-like decorative landscape, is imbued with the omnipresent organic vitality that the artist strove to convey. Its spatial construction is somewhat complex, with a horizon line situated at very top of the painting, revealing a mere glimpse of sky, a tiny cloud...

Still controversial in Norway, Munch met with a favourable reception in Berlin, Prague and Paris, where he exhibited at the Salon des Indépendants in 1903 and 1904. He showed several views of Asgarstrand, a village on the shores of the Oslo fjord. *Summer Night at Asgarstrand* is boldly structured by simplified geometric forms, slashed by a long diagonal and enlivened with contrasting colours. In

André Derain
1880-1954
Charing Cross Bridge
1906
Oil on canvas
81 x 100 cm
Max and Rosy
Kaganovitch donation,
1973

Gustav Klimt
1862-1918
*Rosebushes under
the Trees*
1905
Oil on canvas
110 x 115 cm
Purchased in 1980

Giovanni Giacometti
1868-1933
View of Capolago (Tessin)
Circa 1907
Oil on canvas
51.5 x 60 cm
Purchased courtesy
of Philippe Meyer, 1997

Sweden, the works of Eugène Jansson were steeped in mystery and anguish. Both Stockholm and its dormitory suburban "barracks" inhabited by the poor seem ready to explode into flames under pressure from an inner fire, a feeling heightened by nervous, swirling brushwork, the fluid use of colour dominated by blues, the tempestuous sky and the branches of the tree blown upwards by the storm (*Proletarian Lodgings*, 1898). The same sense of anguish can be found in August Strindberg's aggressive, dramatic writings.

In Switzerland, landscape painting was also undergoing regeneration. In *Winter Landscape* (1904), a quasi-metaphysical work, Cuno Amiet filled the immense foreground with a stretch of non-monochromatic white, across which a skier has left a trail, rather like a thread upon the snow. Rejecting all notion of the picturesque, and varying his brushwork, Ferdinand Hodler transcribed the eternal force of *The Peak of Mount Andey, near Bonneville* (1909), while Giovanni Giacometti, Alberto and Diego Giacometti's father, produced a revolutionary image in his *View of Capolago* (circa 1907), establishing a climactic tension between the desire to reproduce a landscape and a radical use of colour, applied in juxtaposed bands.

Cuno Amiet
1868-1961
Snowy Landscape
also known as *Grosser Winter (Midwinter)*
1904
Oil on canvas
178 x 235 cm
Purchased with the participation of the Meyer Foundation and private sponsors in memory of Maurice and Betty Robin, 1999

Edvard Munch
1863-1944
Summer Night
at Asgarstrand
1904
Oil on canvas
99 x 103 cm
Purchased in 1986

Sculpture

Previous page
Auguste Rodin
1840-1917
The Walking Man
1905
213 x 161 x 72 cm
Donated by Maurice
Fenaille, Victor de
Goloubeff, Joanny Peytel
and Léon Grunbaum, 1911

Sculpture during the Second Empire was alive with many different schools of thought: Romanticism, a return to strict Classicism or the elegant agility of the Renaissance - an eclecticism which took delight in mingling different influences and diversifying materials. Soaring above them all was the powerful, dynamic talent of Jean-Baptiste Carpeaux, whose oeuvre dominated the field for quarter of a century.

Romanticism first appeared in sculpture in the 1830s, and its goal was expressiveness rather than purity of form. To achieve expression, sculptors readily distorted proportions and modelling, introducing vigorous movement and strong contrasts. The most Romantic sculptor of all was Augustin Préault, who grandly proclaimed: "I am not for the finite, I am for the infinite." His *Ophelia* is almost more literary than sculptural (given its Shakespearean subject), accentuating transience, emotion and death, and refusing to delineate form. Barye, whose haughty lion guards the gates to the museum, was a Romantic, too, using a powerfully classical style to carve manly allegories for the new Louvre (*Force, War, Order, Peace*, 1855, plaster). Napoleon had the fibre of the Romantic hero, and Napoleonic history and legend were a major source of inspiration for painters and sculptors. *Napoleon Waking up to Immortality*, commissioned by Noisot, a fervent Bonapartist and the former commander of the grenadiers on Elbe, conjures up a vision from beyond the grave: the Emperor, emerging from his shroud, awakens to his hour of glory (the bronze version is in Fixin, near Dijon). Even in the essentially Classical work of James Pradier there is a Romantic tinge: although *Sappho's* clothing and face conform to Classical canons, the subject matter and the figure's melancholic posture betray a different spirit.

Alongside this Romantic trend, the Classical tradition gave rise to a return to an almost archaeological strictness. This movement is illustrated by Pierre-Jules Cavelier and his group *Cornelia, Mother of the Gracchi,* and by Eugène Guillaume, who persisted in the cult of antiquity to the end of his career. *The Cenotaph of the Gracchi* is true to a type of funerary monument that was common under the Republic and at the beginning of the Roman Empire, periods which generated the myth of the virile, pure Roman. *The Reaper,* a bronze dating from 1849, uses the same pose as the *Borghese Gladiator,* a famous Hellenistic statue now in the Louvre, which the sculptor tried to adapt to a less belligerent task! Gabriel Jules Thomas produced a pensive, inspired *Virgil* for the Cour Carrée in the Louvre; the finished statue was considered too handsome for the courtyard and was allocated to the Luxembourg Gardens.

One group of artists stands out among the many movements in this eclectic period: Alexandre Falguière, Paul Dubois, Antonin Mercié and Hippolyte Moulin, all particularly attracted by the elegant art of the Renaissance, which earned them the nickname "the Florentines". It would be fair to add Ernest Christophe, whose *Human Comedy*, "an allegorical statue in Renaissance style", inspired Baudelaire's poem *The Mask* (*Les Fleurs du Mal – 20*).

Auguste Préault
1809-1879
Ophelia
1842-1876
Bronze relief
75 x 200 x 20 cm

Eugène Guillaume
1822-1905
Cenotaph of the Gracchi
1848-1853
Bronze
85 x 90 cm

James Pradier
1790-1852
Sappho
Salon of 1852
Marble
118 x 70 cm
Purchased by Napoleon III
at the Salon of 1852

François Rude
1784-1855
*Napoleon Waking up to
Immortality*
1846
Original plaster model
215 x 195 cm

Ernest Carrier-Belleuse, who was similarly strongly inspired by the Renaissance and the eighteenth century, sometimes turned to Antiquity, as is seen in his group *Hebe* (marble, 1869); the same could be said of *The Victor of the Cockfight* by Falguière and *A Find in Pompeii*, by Moulin. The latter's precise, harmonious style shows the appeal of the Hellenistic bronzes found in Pompeii as well as the importance of *Mercury* by Jean de Bologne (1529-1608), seen in the studied attempt to give the figures rhythm and balance. Mercié, too, was a fervent admirer of Tuscan sculpture (*David*, bronze, 1872). *Woman Bitten by a Snake*, marble, by Auguste Clésinger, sparked a scandal at the 1872 Salon; the model, Apollonie Sabatier, who was Baudelaire's "Présidente", "muse and Madonna", unveiled all the secrets of her anatomy since the statue was cast from life before being carved in marble. Her face, however, was not cast and the smooth, idealised features fit uneasily on a body shown with pitiless realism!

The Second Empire discovered polychromy through the Greek or Roman sculptures still bearing traces of paint that were send back to France by architects and sculptors studying at the French Academy in Rome, and through publications such as the works of the architect Jacques Ignace Hittorf. One of the prime movers in the revival of polychromy was Charles Cordier, who was attracted by ethnography, fascinated by the potential of the onyx quarries in Algeria, and an enthusiastic supporter of the European vogue for the Orient. *The Sudanese Negro* attempts to portray a typical individual in the most authentic costume. This taste for pomp was perfectly in tune with the mentality of the Second Empire, and reached its height in Charles Garnier's Opera House, a triumph of architecture and polychrome sculpture.

Alexandre Falguière
1831-1900
*The Victor of the
Cockfight*
1864
Bronze
174 x 100 cm

Hippolyte Moulin
1832-1884
A Find in Pompeii
1863
Bronze
187 x 64 cm

Antonin Mercié
1845-1916
David
1872
Bronze
184 x 76 cm

Charles Cordier
1827-1905
Sudanese Negro
1857
Bronze and onyx
96 x 66 cm
Purchased by Napoleon III
at the Salon of 1857

Jean-Baptiste
Known as **Auguste**
Clésinger
1814-1883
Woman Bitten by a Snake
Salon de 1847
Marble
56.5 x 180 cm

Jean-Baptiste Carpeaux
1827-1875
Ugolino
1860
Terracotta
56 x 41.5 cm

"When I recognised my own appearance in the four faces, I gnawed my hands with grief, and my children, thinking it was for hunger, leapt to their feet crying: 'Oh, Father! We will not be so grieved if you eat us...'"

The tragic theme of Ugolino, one of the damned heroes of Dante's *Divine Comedy* (*Inferno, 33*), inspired many Romantic and Symbolist artists, from Delacroix to Rodin. It is a terrible subject, telling the story of Count Ugolino della Gherardesca, a tyrant in Pisa in the thirteenth century, who was locked up with his children and grandchildren by his enemy, archbishop Ubaldini, and left to die of hunger, which he did, but, alas, not until he had eaten their flesh.

This group was executed by Jean-Baptiste Carpeaux when he was a resident at the Villa Medici, the seat of the French Academy in Rome. *Ugolino* did not meet the requirements of the Academy: the subject was neither mythological nor Biblical; the work included several figures and could not be produced in a single year. But the theme and Carpeaux's preliminary studies in 1858 aroused such interest that he was granted a dispensation. Carpeaux first thought of a low-relief and his preliminary research shows the influence of Michelangelo, whose work he admired and had studied closely, especially *The Last Judgement*. But Dante and Michelangelo had been linked in the artist's mind for many years: "A statue designed by the poet of *The Divine Comedy* and sculpted by the father of Moses, would be a masterpiece of the human spirit," he wrote in 1854, the year he won the Prix de Rome, after ten years as a student at the Ecole des Beaux-Arts working first with François Rude and then with Joseph Duret.

It was during a trip to Paris in 1860 that Carpeaux made the terracotta model in the display case, in which a fourth child appears. The plaster cast (Musée du Petit Palais, Paris) was finished in November 1861 and was acclaimed when exhibited in Rome, but turned down by the Paris Institute. Nonetheless, the bronze was commissioned by the State in 1862 and placed in the Tuileries Gardens.

Carpeaux's career was brief but brilliant, spanning the fifteen years after his Prix de Rome; it is intertwined with the imperial family and high society of his time, as well as with the decoration of the most important public monuments of the Second Empire.

His terracotta or plaster models, marble busts and groups vividly portray Napoleon III and the imperial family. Introduced to court at the Tuileries by Princess Mathilde (a cousin of the Emperor), he tutored the crown prince in drawing and was commissioned to make a full length statue of the boy with his dog. *The Crown Prince and his Dog Nero,* the marble version of which dates to 1865, was preceded by a large number of studies which reveal Carpeaux's gifts: his keen sense of observation and sensitive, vigorous rendering of life. The group was very popular and became widely known through reproductions and reduced models in various materials. This finesse in bringing out the personality of his sitters can also be seen in the busts of friends and contemporaries; thus *Eugenie Fiocre*, plaster, 1869, heightens the elegance of the young woman, who was a first dancer at the Opera, and echoes the eighteenth-century tradition in its concern for presence and decorative effect.

During the Second Empire, the capital was turned into one huge construction site: "Paris has been slashed with a sabre, her open veins feeding a hundred thousand road workers and masons" (Zola). Commissions were plentiful. Carpeaux was asked to decorate the side of the Pavillon de Flore (1863-1866)

Jean-Baptiste Carpeaux
1827-1875
Ugolino
1862
Bronze
194 x 148 cm

Jean-Baptiste Carpeaux
1827-1875
*The Crown Prince and his
Dog, Nero*
1865
Marble
140 x 65.4 cm

Jean-Baptiste Carpeaux
1827-1875
Palombella
(Barbara Pasquarelli)
Terracotta bust
40.2 x 26.5 cm
Holfeld bequest, 1967

Jean-Baptiste Carpeaux
1827-1875
Eugénie Fiocre
1869
Plaster
83 x 51 cm

Jean-Baptiste Carpeaux
1827-1875
*Imperial France
Protecting Agriculture
and Science*
1863-1866
Patinated plaster
268 x 427 cm

that faced the Seine in the new Louvre remodelled by Lefuel. The pavilion was crowned with an allegorical group: *Imperial France Protecting Agriculture and the Sciences*, the composition of which is reminiscent of Michelangelo's work in the Medici Chapel in Florence. Above it, testifying to the sculptor's discovery of the fleshy beauties of Rubens and the Flemish painters, a ring of prancing children glorifies *The Triumph of Flora*, in an animated composition characteristic of Carpeaux. But a sulphurous scandal engulfed Carpeaux with *Dance*, commissioned in 1863 by the architect Charles Garnier for his new Opera House.

It took Carpeaux three years to settle on his theme of a ring of five figures around a leaping male spirit, which makes the relief "spring off the wall". Finally numbering nine figures, the work was unveiled in 1869 and triggered a scandal. It was called a "vile Saturnalia" and an "insult to public morality", and the sculptor Achille Gumery was asked to make another group (Musée des Beaux-Arts, Angers). The outbreak of war in 1870, then the death of Carpeaux, saved his group from destruction. Eroded by the Paris air, *Dance* was put in the Louvre in 1964 and a copy by Paul Belmondo replaced it on the Opera House. The same circular pattern is found in one of Carpeaux's last great works, the fountain of the *Four Parts of the World*, for the Observatory Gardens. The subject presents the four cardinal points (the horses springing out of the water at the edge of the fountain were sculpted by Emmanuel Fremiet). Rejecting the static poses usually found in this type of representation, Carpeaux chose to show "the four cardinal points turning as if to follow the rotation of the earth, so that I have one front view, one three quarter view, one side view and one back view." He even wanted to give the figures a patina to match the skin colour of the different races but the idea was ruled out.

Jean-Baptiste Carpeaux
1827-1875
The Four Parts of the World Holding a Celestial Sphere
1867-1872
Plaster
280 x 177 cm

Jean-Baptiste Carpeaux
1827-1875
Dance
1869
Echaillon stone
420 x 298 cm

Honoré Daumier
Ernest Meissonier

Honoré Daumier has a special place in his generation, forming a link between Romanticism and Realism. He was a man of many talents who was not only a great painter, a keenly skilled and expressive sculptor but also an excellent draughtsman and lithographer.

Daumier's sculptures were often a starting point for his paintings or drawings; this was the case for the *Parliamentarians (Celebrities of the Middle Path)*, a series of thirty-six clay busts coloured with oils. The caricatures published in the aptly named review *La Caricature* were drawn from these busts after 1831, and it was for the magazine's director, Charles Philippon, who also founded *Le Charivari* in 1832, that Daumier exercised his talent as a caricaturist. He used distortion and exaggeration to expose deep-seated truths in people, who appear as universal types; polychromy accentuates features, pitilessly revealing defects and tics. Bronze reproductions of these busts were made between 1927 and 1953 in varying quantities depending on the busts selected (the Musée des Beaux-Arts, Marseilles, owns a complete set). *The Emigrants,* plaster relief, 1848, shows Daumier's broad, sweeping, powerful technique and his skill in manipulating mass and form. The strength and movement that bring this group alive give one of his favourite themes a timeless quality. *The Fugitives* gives the impression of a downtrodden, anxious crowd hastening by... Lastly, *Ratapoil (Ratskin),* bronze 1850, who became the symbol of Napoleon's soldiers laid off on half-pay by the Restoration vengefully preparing the advent of Napoleon III, brought out Daumier's Baroque, expressionist talent

It was not until much later, when he was nearly forty, that Daumier began his career as a painter, entering a contest run by the short-lived Second Republic in 1848.

Ernest Meissonier, a keen history painter, very convincingly imitated the real world with his astonishing polychrome wax figure of *The Traveller,* going so far as to dress his figurine in cloth and to fashion a metal bit and leather reins for the horse, which is modelled over a miniature skeleton.

Honoré Daumier
The Fugitives
Circa 1850-1852
Fragment of the first
state
Plaster relief

Honoré Daumier
1808-1879
Celebrities of the Middle Path or The Parliamentarians
Clay coloured with oils

Purchased with the aid of Michel David-Weill and the Fondation Lutèce, 1980

Jean Vatout
Deputato
20 x 16 cm

Laurent Cunin, known as Cunin-Gridaine
or *Wicked Man*
Politician
15 x 13 cm

Charles Léonard Gallois
or *The Ironist*
Republican public law specialist and historian
21 x 13 cm

Jean-Auguste Chevandier de Valdrome or *The Fool*
Member of Parliament
19 x 14 cm

Jean Claude Fulchiron
or *The Hypocrite*
Poet and Member of Parliament
17 x 12 cm

Félix Barthe
Magistrate
17 x 15 cm

François Guizot
or *The Bore*
Minister of the Interior
22 x 17 cm

Count François Dominique Reynaud de Montlosier
or *The Sly Fox*
19 x 15 cm

Ernest Meissonier
1815-1891
Traveller in the Wind
Red and grey wax, fabric and leather
47 x 60 x 39.5 cm

Edgar Degas

Degas started sculpting in 1881 but just for himself, as he said: "It is for my own satisfaction that I shaped beasts and people out of wax, not to have a rest from painting or drawing, but to give my paintings and drawings more expression, more ardour and life... They are warm up exercises, documents, no more." When Degas died, his close friend the sculptor Albert Bartholomé found nearly 150 wax or clay sculptures in his studio; 73 were restored then cast in bronze by A. Hébrard. Twenty-five copies were to be made of each model, according to the terms of a contract dated 13 May 1918. Degas made a meticulous study of movement in his series on *Horses,* with the help of Muybridge's analytical photographs, whereas he treated *Dancers* and *Women at their Toilette* in a free, spontaneous manner. *The Bath Tub* is one of his most original compositions, which has to be viewed from above to understand its interlocking forms; the model is lying in a wide, shallow tub, with her left hand laid on the rim. The wax figure of a *Little Dancer, Aged Fourteen,* complete with doll's hair, tutu and dancing slippers, horrified the public. However, at the Impressionist exhibition of 1881, Karl-Joris Huysmans, who was struck by its "terrible reality", saw it as "the only really modern work I have seen in sculpture."

Edgar Degas
1834-1917
Horse with Head Lowered
Bronze
48.6 x 95 cm
Purchased in 1930 with
the aid of the heirs of
Degas and the foundry
owner A.A. Hébrard

Edgar Degas
1834-1917
Study for a Spanish Dance
1896-1911
Original wax
45.2 x 21 x 195 cm
Gift from Paul Mellon through the Foundation

for French Museums, for the Musée d'Orsay's fifth anniversary, in memory of his friend, the ambassador Emmanuel de Margerie (1992)

Edgar Degas
1834-1917
Little Dancer, Aged Fourteen
1879-1881
Patinated bronze, muslin skirt, satin ribbon

98 x 35.2 x 24.5 cm
Purchased in 1930 with the aid of the heirs of Degas and the foundry owner A.A. Hébrard

Edgar Degas
1834-1917
The Bathtub
1888-1889
Bronze
22.5 x 43.8 x 45.8 cm
Purchased in 1930 with the aid of the heirs of Degas and the foundry owner A.A. Hébrard

Driven by a "terrible itch for the unknown", Gauguin's life is a sort of endless journey which took him several times from Brittany to the Pacific, the two main poles in his life. Unwilling to confine himself to one technique he tried them all, even ceramics and burnt earthenware.

Symbolist influences appear in his highly original wooden sculptures; designed as the companion piece for *Love and You will be Happy*, 1889 (Boston, Museum of Fine Arts), the low relief *Be Mysterious* shows that Gauguin wants to regain the freshness of the lesson he learnt from the so called primitive arts. Executed in Brittany in 1890, it reveals influences from Japanese prints and Art Nouveau. The beauty of the wood and the carving makes it one of the majestic works of his pre-Tahitian sculpture.

When he arrived in Tahiti, in 1891, he discovered the mysteries of the Maori pantheon. At Mataeia, he lived with Tehura, the vahine whose features he carved, expressing his admiration for "the most beautiful race in the world"; he established a sort of synthesis between this smooth, stylised face and the rough-hewn "exotic Eve" on the back of the piece. His idols, which he called "savage trinkets", were dictated to him by Tahitian mythology. *Idol with a Shell*, carved out of ironwood, uses extremely diverse materials; the back of the piece is strongly influenced by traditional Marquesan tikis. Many of his sculptures are utilitarian objects, canes or bowls decorated with Marquesan motifs.

Oviri, "the killer", as Gauguin called the savage god which presided over death and mourning, is his largest ceramic piece. He was particularly attached

Paul Gauguin
1848-1903
Be Mysterious
1890
Wood
73 x 95 cm

Paul Gauguin
  1848-1903
  Idol with a Shell
  Ironwood (pua),
  mother-of-pearl, ivory
  1892-1893
  34.4 x 14.8 cm

Purchased with the aid of
Mme Huc de Monfreid
(with a life interest), 1951

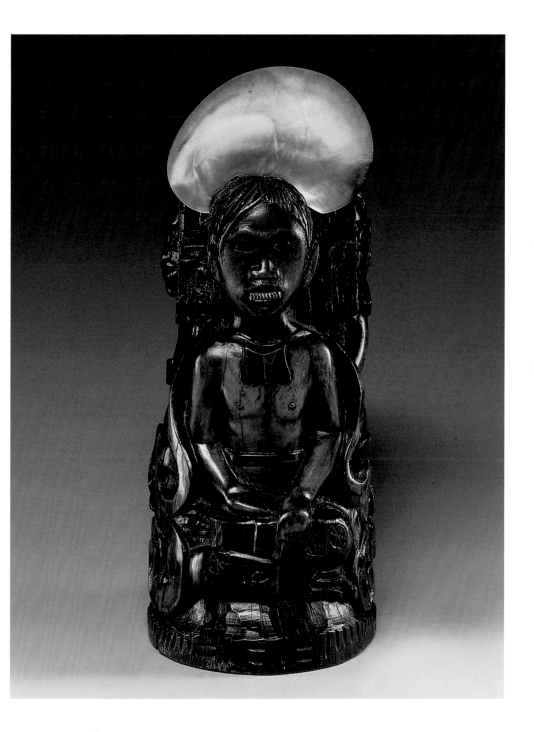

to this powerful work, which emanates mystery and strangeness, and wanted it to be put on his grave.

In September 1901, he "set off for a simpler country, and new wilder things", Hiva Oa, an island in the Marquesas. Gauguin bought a piece of land from the bishop there, to build a big hut on piles from wood, palms and bamboo. He carved the uprights from imported sequoia timber and gave it the provocative name of *Maison du jouir.* After his death on 8 May 1903, the five panels were put up for sale in Tahiti. Victor Ségalen, a young naval doctor at the time, bought four of the panels as a gift for the poet Saint-Paul Roux. They became part of the national French collection in 1952, and the purchase of the fifth panel, in 1990, has endowed the Musée d'Orsay with the most important set of decorative carving by Gauguin.

Paul Gauguin
1848-1903
Oviri
1894
Partly enamelled
earthenware
75 x 19 cm

Georges Lacombe
1868-1916
Isis
1893-1894
Mahogany relief partly
in polychromy
115 x 62 cm

Paul Gauguin
1848-1903
Maison du jouir
1901
Polychrome relief
in sequoia wood
240 x 562 cm

The Third Republic

The proclamation of the Republic on 4 September 1870 did not cause a sudden change of style. The sponsorship of the republican state replaced imperial commissions in the diffusion of an ideal which needed traditional iconography to be understood. Some works recalled the Franco-Prussian War and the Commune; hence the desolate mood of Paul Cabet's allegory (*Eighteen Hundred and Seventy Seven*, 1877, marble), or Henri Chapu's *Joan of Arc*, which was meant to revive hope, the insolence of Mercié's *Gloria Victis*, and the promise of revenge that emerged with Falguière's *Resistance* and *The Defence of Paris*. The Republic launched public competitions to impose its image through monuments, allegorical busts and medals.

Sculptures continued to invade the city! Public monuments, festival decors, busts and statues to the glory of national heroes sprang up all over Paris. The *Monument to Gambetta* by the sculptor Aubé (the terracotta model entered in the 1884 competition is on display in the museum) was erected in the Napoleon Courtyard of the Louvre. It was later dismantled; the bronze was melted down during the Occupation and the stones were removed in 1954. This model is very educational; the tableau and the inscriptions vie with one another in the demonstration.

Jean-Léon Gérôme, a painter and sculptor, celebrated Greek beauty in his *Tanagra,* which created a sensation in the 1890 Salon. The polychrome decoration he added at the time has since disappeared. Gérôme's idea was to recall painted antique statues, whereas Louis-Ernest Barrias showed a taste for mixed media (already developed by Cordier during the Second Empire), by assembling coloured marble, onyx, lapis lazuli and malachite in his allegory of *Nature Unveiled Before Science*. René de Saint Marceaux's *Spirit Guarding the Tomb* and Victor Segoffin's *War Dance* achieve strength and power in their Baroque search for movement. History, mythology and allegory were all pretexts for the female

Jean-Léon Gérôme
1824-1904
Tanagra
1890
Marble
154.7 x 56 cm

Victor Ségoffin
1867-1925
War Dance
or Sacred Dance
1903-1905
Marble
250 x 140 cm

Louis-Ernest Barrias
1841-1905
Nature Unveiled Before
Science
1899
Polychrome marble and
Algerian onyx
200 x 85 cm

Charles-René
de Saint-Marceaux
1845-1915
Spirit Guarding the Tomb
1879
Marble
168.5 x 95 cm

Paul Troubetzkoy
1866-1938
Robert de Montesquiou
(1855-1921)
1907
Bronze
56 x 62 cm

Jean-Léon Gérôme
1824-1904
Aimé Morot
1850-1913
Monument to Gérôme.
Gérôme Sculpting 'The
Gladiators'
1878 and 1909
Bronze
360 x 182 x 170 cm

nudes so prized by the art market (*Youth,* 1885, marble, by Antonin Carlès; *Eve,* 1891, marble by Eugène Delaplanche).

There were some excellent portraits of society figures; thus the Russian artist Troubetzkoy executed a bronze statue of Robert de Montesquiou, a Symbolist writer, aesthete and man of the world; he is sitting, "with his head held high, a dominating gaze, his right hand resting on a cane supporting his outstretched arm, a broad-brimmed hat held in his left hand and a coat draped over his arm, the line of the folds extended by the long body of a fine Russian hound..."

The same quest for the Baroque can be seen in monumental sculpture, characterised by sweeping gestures and exaggerated expressions. Commissioned to decorate the outside of the palaeontology gallery of the Muséum d'Histoire Naturelle, built by the architect Ferdinand Dutert in 1894-1895, Barrias and Coutan designed high reliefs illustrating the wild, brutish life of early Man (*Alligator Hunters* or *The Nubians,* 1894, plaster by Barrias; *The Eagle Hunters,* 1900, plaster by Coutan). The original models for the bronzes on the front of the Muséum are on display here.

Gustave Deloye, too, had Baroque references but his preference was for the tormented, theatrical Baroque of Central Europe which he had visited; his strangely composed *St. Mark* group is full of the feverish grandiloquence that took hold of sculptors at the end of the century.

Fremiet is part of the historical realism movement, as his large *St. Michael* amply illustrates. It is a beaten copper replica of the weather vane banner that has crowned Mont Saint Michel since 1897. It shows a keen respect for traditional iconography and meticulous rendering of the armour. The plaster, presented in the 1896 Salon, was cast by Monduit, a firm which produced and sold cast iron art works and built an international reputation for fine, solid work that faithfully reproduced the sculptor's model. The generosity of Madame G. Pasquier-Monduit has given the Musée d'Orsay this masterpiece and a valuable set of drawings and rich documentation on the firm, which also cast the quadrigas on the Grand Palais, many of the elements of the Alexander III bridge, Frédéric Bartholdi's *Statue of Liberty,* in New York, and the *Belfort Lion.*

The taste for reality and historical truth taken to the extreme is found in the astonishing group *The Gladiators.* The statue made by the painter Gérôme was long thought to have been lost; in fact, it was used by his son-in-law, Aimé Morot, himself a painter and sculptor, to pay homage to Gérôme, whom he portrayed in the process of sculpting *The Gladiators,* integrating Gérôme's original work in his own composition!

Emmanuel Fremiet
1824-1910
St. Michael
Beaten copper
617 x 260 cm
Gift from Mme G. Pasquier
Monduit ; on loan from the
Monuments Historiques

Jules Dalou
Constantin Meunier

First painting and then sculpture rediscovered the qualities of realism which has always been part of the French tradition: Vicenzo Vela in Italy, Constantin Meunier in Belgium and Jules Dalou in France turned to the workers and peasants around them and used them as the subject of works that were stripped of all historical, mythological and religious trappings.

Dalou, who expressed his sympathy for the Republican Party in the passionate bust of *Henri Rochefort* (1888, bronze) had taken an active part in the Paris Commune. He managed to flee to England with his family, so it was from London that he sent his project for the *Triumph of the Republic*, in 1879, the year that the armistice was signed. *The Blacksmith* (1879-1880, plaster) pushing the cartwheel is wearing clogs and an apron and carrying a sledge hammer on his shoulder. Nobody could take him for Vulcan; he is the future hero of the *Monument to Labour*. The monument was never produced although Dalou accumulated sketches and projects after 1889 and completed *The Big Peasant* (1898-1899, bronze).

Although his interest in everyday reality is apparent in his choice of subjects – women at their toilette, workers – it also shows through in his skilled modelling, which refuses any concession to the idealism of academic art: the terracotta nude study for the *Republic* shows all the strengths and weaknesses of a body which belongs to a woman before becoming an allegory.

Constantin Meunier showed a keener interest in life in the pit, the dockers in the ports, the peasants in all their coarseness - indeed in industry, the crucible of human labour but also the source of the economic boom that was revolutionising Europe! Aware of the force that the workers represented – symbolised by his *Docker in the Port of Antwerp* (1890, bronze) – he endowed them with a dignity and monumentality which made them the equals of mythological heroes. From 1885-1890 on, he too began to dream of a *Monument to Labour*, but he did not finish it until 1929-1930. While working on the project, he produced numerous reliefs showing the *Human Machine* (1902, bronze) that Bernard Hoetger, in turn, used for a powerful composition.

Bernhard Hoetger
1874-1949
Human Machine
1902
Bronze
44 x 37.5 cm
Gift from Mme Marcel
Duchamp, 1977 ; on loan
from the MNAM

Constantin Meunier
1831-1905
The Puddlers
1893
Bronze
50 x 49 cm

Jules Dalou
1838-1902
The Blacksmith
(one of the figures from a
project for a monument:
Triumph of the Republic)
1879-1889

Plaster
67 x 37 cm
Gift from Auguste Biaggi,
a pupil of Dalou, 1952

Auguste Rodin

Auguste Rodin
1840-1917
Winter
1890
Marble
Gift from Robert-Gérard
family, 1996

Rodin holds a major place in the history of nineteenth-century sculpture. His development can be followed from *The Age of Bronze* – which looked so natural that, when he exhibited it at the 1877 Salon, he was accused of having cast his model from life – to the *Muse* intended for a *Monument to Whistler*, 1902, very freely designed, with the parts scarcely joined together and drapery simply dipped in plaster.

After *The Age of Bronze, John the Baptist,* and *Walking Man,* (an enlargement in 1905 of a study executed about 1877-78 for *St John,* - a technique often used by Rodin), a gallery of busts demonstrates his skill as a portraitist. Society figures mingle with artists and literary personalities: opposite the elegant figure of *Madame Vicuña*, wife of the Chilean ambassador in Paris, the symbolist portrait of Camille Claudel, *Thought,* and the heroic busts of *Hugo* and *Rochefort,* stand the famous mask of *The Man with a Broken Nose* and a series of personalities from the art world, critics such as Gustave Geffroy, or artists such as *Pierre Puvis de Chavannes, Eugène Guillaume, Jean-Paul Laurens,* and lastly *Jules Dalou,* a bare-chested figure in which Rodin's rigorous design and precise modelling betray his admiration for the Florentine Renaissance.

From 1880 to 1890 Rodin worked on *The Gates of Hell,* commissioned by the state in 1880 for a museum of the decorative arts which was to have been built on the ruins of the Cour des Comptes – the future site of the Orsay Station. Taking Dante's *Divine Comedy* as its theme, and inspired by the doors of the Baptistery in Florence, it was modelled in fragments, most of which became statues in their own right (*The Thinker, The Kiss, Fugit Amor, Shades...*). In this tangle of bodies that passion was sweeping into the abyss, "gasping, anxious, meaningful figures, full of pathetic clamour", the two main episodes gave rise to, left, the entwined couple of Paolo and Francesca, the original for *The Kiss,* and, its companion piece on the right, the figures of *Ugolino* and his children who, slightly modified and enlarged in 1906, and wrapped in drapery that can be seen under the plaster, became the group displayed nearby.

Rodin took his inspiration from Canto 33 of the Inferno: "...I betook me, now grown blind, to grope over them all, and for three days aloud call'd on them who were dead. Then fasting got the mastery of grief." Not far from the *Gates,* is *Fugit Amor,* taken from one of them. The young man carried by a woman in a desperate race, seems to be Rodin's answer to Camille Claudel's *The Age of Maturity:* executed at the time they broke up, the later group symbolises the master's hesitation between his ageing mistress, Rose Beuret, who wins the day, and Camille, who, as *The Imploring Woman,* is toppling over in her effort to retain him. The three figures are set on a terrace that curves like a wave and echoes the sinuous lines of Art Nouveau work, which is displayed in the last rooms with a cupola ceiling.

Winter (1890), is the only marble version of a theme already handled by Rodin and Jules Desbois. The bronze, acquired by the State in 1891, is on display at the Musée Rodin, under the title *She who was the helmet-maker's beautiful wife* from the poem by François Villon. The generosity of Robert Gérard's family endowed the museum in 1996 with this "horribly beautiful thing", a painfully poignant image of decrepitude... This image of old age is accompanied by a terracotta sketch, *Misery* by Desbois, the inventor of the theme and the model, and by the knotted, emaciated plaster torso of *Clotho* by Camille Claudel.

Auguste Rodin
1840-1917
Thought
(a portrait of Camille
Claudel)
1886-1889
Marble
74 x 55 cm

Auguste Rodin
1840-1917
Mme Vicuña
1888
Marble
57 x 49 cm

Camille Claudel
1864-1943
The Age of Maturity
1893-1903
Bronze
114 x 163 cm

Yet Rodin turned to a more abstract art with his *Balzac*. The Société des Gens de Lettres wanted to erect a monument to the man who had been its second chairman. After the death of Henri Chapu, who was first given the task, Zola saw to it that Rodin received the commission. Starting from realistic – or visionary? – studies of the nude, that both simplified and distorted his subject (Rodin believing that "modern sculpture must exaggerate forms, from a moral point of view"), he finished up with a pyramidal silhouette designed to accentuate the outsized head. The statue was an almost abstract symbol of the novelist's force, giving new impetus to the idea of a public monument which until then was supposed to give a precise description, surrounded by allegories, of the person in whose honour it had been raised. The plaster model sparked such a scandal at the 1898 Salon that the commission was taken away from Rodin and given to Falguière. Although it was not put in its present location (Boulevard Raspail, Paris) until 1939, *Balzac* is now regarded as one of the works that paved the way for the twentieth century.

Auguste Rodin
1840-1917
Balzac
1898
Plaster
275 x 121 cm
On loan from the Musée Rodin

Auguste Rodin
1840-1917
The Gates of Hell
1880-1917
Plaster
625 x 400 cm
On loan from the Musée
Rodin

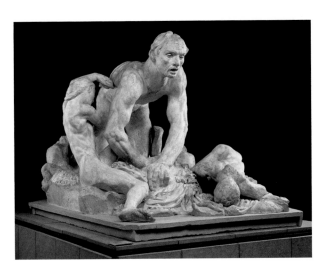

Auguste Rodin
1840-1917
Ugolino
1882
Plaster
140 x 140 cm
On loan from the Musée
Rodin

Mystery, strangeness and uncertainty are attractive themes for artists; Pierre Roche's *Morgane the Fay,* Rupert Carabin's witch immobilised by the angelus (*Légende savernoise*), and Félix Fix-Masseau's *The Secret* all interpret various eternal myths and legends that nourish human imagination.

The mask which hides or, on the contrary, reveals the mystery of human beings is the preserve of Jean Carriès, who fashioned them in clay or bronze. Albert Bartholomé's mask was inspired by his Japanese model *Tadamasa Hayashi,* who was part of his country's official delegation in 1905 and became the leading ambassador for Japanese art in France. This bronze head, with its fine red patina, suggests the masks used in Nô theatre, but also seeks to give a true likeness.

The German sculptor Max Klinger gives Cassandra, the unhappy prophetess whom nobody would ever believe, a tense attitude and glowing cornelian eyes presaging the fire that would soon destroy her native Troy. The Belgian Georges Minne portrays distress and destitution through the thin, naked body of his *Boy Kneeling at the Spring,* while *The Sphinx* by the Polish sculptor Boleslas Biegas seems to be a pitiless incarnation of death and desperation. The English artist Alfred Drury incarnates *The Spirit of the Night* in a head with closed eyes and a pensive, spiritual expression.

Albert Bartholomé attains universal symbolism with a moderation and style that put him at the opposite end of the scale from Rodin; his *Monument to the Dead in Père Lachaise,* (1889-1899) is a "shadowy mouth" ready to swallow up all who those who come near.

In Rodin's eyes, far from having a best angle, a sculpture is the sum of all the profiles created by the light falling on the model. Medardo Rosso, the sculptor whose work has the most in common with the Impressionist painters, took this idea to the extreme and tried to suggest the atmosphere that surrounded his figures by disintegrating their shape: in *Ecce Puer, a Portrait of Alfred Mond at the Age of Six* the face has been smoothed by the light.

Albert Bartholomé
1848-1928
Tadamasa Hayashi
(1856-1906)
1892
Bronze mask
25.5 x 19 x cm
Gift from the Société des
Amis du Musée d'Orsay
(1990)

Boleslas Biegas
1877-1954
The Sphinx
1902
Plaster
46 x 39 cm

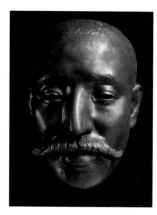

Georges Minne
1866-1941
Boy Kneeling at the
Spring
1898
Bronze
785 x 19 cm
Gift from Enrique Mistler,
1933

Max Klinger
1857-1920
Cassandra,
1886-1900
Bronze and cornelian
59 x 32 cm

Medardo Rosso
1858-1928
Ecce Puer
1906
Bronze
44 x 37 cm

Rodin was surrounded by many practising artists, several of whom later led an independent career. Some, like Desbois, never shook off the master's influence. On the other hand, Lucien Schnegg and Antoine Bourdelle became part of the movement which, in the early twentieth century, tried to find the force, balance and clarity epitomised by antique sculpture. Bartholomé was considered the precursor of this movement and his efforts to achieve rhythm are tinged with Neo-Hellenism (*Monument to Jean Jacques Rousseau*).

Bourdelle too applied the "brake of style" and in the early twentieth century he put a stop to the expressive romanticism of his youth, which can still be felt in *Head of a Fighting Man*, reused in 1905 in the *Monument to the Dead* in Montauban. He made archaism into a real discipline, executing *Head of Apollo* (1900-1909), *Penelope* (1905-1908) dreamily graceful despite her monumentality and, above all, *Hercules the Archer* (1909) in which he shows extraordinary skill in composition, the distribution of empty space and the portrayal of tension. "The unbelievably daring movement of this archer poised in midair, his foot pressed against a rocky spur, this man who seems to be leaping in his very stillness, this summary, judicious modelling, full and vibrant, is one of the most prodigious attempts in living art. Realism here verges on idealism."

Emile Antoine Bourdelle
1861-1929
Apollo
1909
Gilt bronze
67.4 x 27.2 cm
Accepted in lieu of
inheritance tax in 1989

Emile Antoine Bourdelle
1861-1929
Hercules the Archer
1909-1923
Gilt bronze
248 x 247 cm

After a period as a painter, weaver and ceramist, Maillol turned to sculpture about 1895. Although the undulating lines of the *Dancer* that he executed at that time are reminiscent of the animated forms of Art Nouveau, he soon developed a more austere style, as can be seen in the *Two Bathers*.

In 1900, he began the first of his great figures, *The Mediterranean.* The model which served to make the marble statue now in the Musée d'Orsay was exhibited at the Salon d'Automne in 1905. A comparison between the final state and the more naturalistic large study, in 1902, reveals the artist's approach. "It is not enough to have a model and copy it," he said. "Nature undeniably underlies the work... But art is not a matter of copying nature." Putting the emphasis on a particular point of view, he simplified modelling and composition: no parallel limbs, no twisting, but a geometrical framework that seems self-evident. The relief *Desire* (1907) is an admirable example of this quest for perfection. For Maillol, beauty lay in the harmony and balance of the passionless gestures of a body perfectly under control.

This way of seeing things led him to do away with the subject and for the *Monument to Cezanne* (1912-1925), refused by the city of Aix en Provence for which it was designed, he produced a draped female figure holding an olive branch, in a Classicism that he felt was the best way to sum up Cézanne.

When he first started to sculpt, Maillol, like Paul Gauguin and Georges Lacombe, worked directly on wood. But it was Joseph Bernard who went a step further, attacking huge blocks of stone or wood to free the nymph imprisoned within. The technique of direct carving, by sweeping away the intermediate steps between the work and the artist, slaked the thirst for force and sincerity experienced by sculptors who were weary of academism. *Straining After Nature* (1906-1907) both in its title and in its massive appearance reveals a desire for close union between form and substance. *Dance* (1911-1913) was executed in the same way, but the desire for simplification is overlaid by a search for rhythm – also apparent in *Water Carrier* (1912) – which brings them close to the works of Maurice Denis.

Joseph Bernard
1866-1931
Straining after Nature
1906
Stone
32 x 23 cm
Gift from Jean Bernard,
the artist's son, 1980

Aristide Maillol
1861–1944
Desire
1907
Lead
120 x 115 cm

Aristide Maillol
1861–1944
Dancer
1895
Pear-tree wood
22 x 24 cm
Mme Thadée Natanson
bequest, 1953

Aristide Maillol
The Mediterranean
1905
Marble
110 x 117 cm

The Decorative Arts

Eclecticism prevailed in the arts applied to industry. This constant call for styles from the past was already present in the Louis-Philippe period, but it was not consolidated until the second half of the nineteenth century, through the establishment of museums and important private collections of historical art, through the works and compendiums of archaeologists, historians, and scholars, and through the emergence of a new clientele, the bourgeoisie, who were not always sure of their judgement and who sought legitimacy and roots. This infatuation for very diverse styles was also stimulated by exploratory travels, colonization, and World Fairs, in which the Western arts were confronted with the arts of the Middle East and Asia.

New industrial corporations surrounded themselves with renowned artists in a desire to unite the Beautiful with the Useful, and Art with Industry; architects, interior decorators, sculptors, painters, and draughtsmen provided designs for original pieces as well as for mass-produced objects. Industrial and commercial art thus contributed to establishing and spreading eclecticism everywhere. *The Washstand of the Duchesse of Parma,* that is, the granddaughter of King Charles X, was one of the first examples of this flourishing eclecticism. Commissioned in 1845 and completed in 1851 to be sent to the World's Fair in London, this piece of furniture made of silver, bronze, and iron, embellished with enamel, niello, and precious stones, is the result of a collaboration between the goldsmith François-Désiré Froment-Meurice, the architect Félix Duban, the sculptors Jean-Jacques Feuchère and Adolphe-Victor Geffroy, known as Geffroy-Dechaume, and the ornamentalist Michel-Joseph Liénard. The set presents a surprising mixture of influences from Islam, the Middle Ages, the Renaissance, and the Baroque style.

With the same aim of an alliance between art and industry, the sculptor Antoine-Louis Barye created various models of ornamental bronzes from the 1840s on, simply patinated for the most part. However, he also realized some richly polychromed pieces at the request of his associate, the engineer Emile Martin, director of the Fourchambault foundry. This was the case for *Tartar Warrior Checking His Horse* (1855), an original version of a patinated bronze model that was widely distributed, as well as the striking mantelpiece ornament of *Roger Carrying off Angelica on the Hippogriff.* The matte, burnished gold accentuates Angelica's delicate nudity and the determined expression on Roger's face, while the polychrome enamel brings out the mane, wings, and tail of the mount, as well as Roger's armour. These magnificent effects owe their existence to Charles Cordier, the master of polychrome sculpture. This spectacular ornament prefigures the series of decorative objects that the big industrial companies Christofle and Barbedienne were to develop between 1860 and 1870, which definitely affirmed the importance of polychromy in bronze works.

Christofle, the first non-religious manufacturer of silverware, underwent unprecedented expansion thanks to their use of galvanic silver-plating, which made it possible to ensure an extensive production of silver-plated metal, all the while maintaining the tradition of luxury silverware. Some exceptional pieces were made for World Fairs, such as *The Education of Achilles Vase,* which mixes reminiscences of mannerism with naturalist motifs of a new spirit, the fruit of a collaboration between the sculptor Mathurin Moreau and the ornamentalist Auguste Madroux.

Antoine-Louis Barye
1796-1875
*Mantelpiece Ornament
with Roger Carrying Off
Angelica on the
Hippogriff and the
Candelabra of the Three
Graces*
1855-1857

Gilt, silvered, and
enamelled bronze, onyx-
marble
59 x 67 x 37 cm
(central group)
95 x 41.5 x 27 cm
(candelabra)
Purchased in 2000

Christofle and Co.
Firm directed by Henri
Bouilhet (1838-1907)
and Paul Christofle
(1830-1910)
*The Education of Achilles
Vase*
1867
Partially gilt silver
H. 75 cm
Purchased in 1982

Ferdinand Barbedienne oversaw the main factory of artistic bronzes and won medals and honorary mentions at international fairs; his art director, Constant Sévin, mainly found inspiration in Renaissance and Hellenistic art (patinated, gilt, or silvered bronze cups, ornamented with fruits, insects, and children). At the 1867 World's Fair, this master ornamentalist presented decorative mirrors of varying modesty and sumptuousness, an example of which is the monumental piece acquired by the museum in 1996. It incorporates figurines by Albert-Ernest Carrier-Belleuse and was produced in an edition of only two copies, which differ in their use of silver-plating, gold-plating, and dark finish. Here, the bronze and gold smith Sévin drew his inspiration from the French Renaissance and from seventeenth-century silver furnishings. In the neo-Greek style, the sculptor and medal maker Ferdinand Levillain designed for Barbedienne the *Medusa* cup (circa 1873), the head of which is accentuated with inlaid eyes and ornate handles, showing a creative interpretation of antique models, and the *Syracuse* cup (circa 1867), which is more austere. The neo-Greek style asserted itself at the end of the Second Empire; the Servant firm, on Rue Vieille-du-Temple, won numerous prizes from international fairs and made a name for itself through its Greek-style bronzes. The sculptor Emile Hébert was the factory's main collaborator; he contributed a sophisticated interpretation of the purest neo-Greek style. The musician terms were derived from a fragmentary marble statue discovered in 1779 and conserved at the British Museum; a cantharus inspired by Hellenistic pieces of gold work, and the circular plaques with an aged golden finish relating the episodes of Dionysos's childhood, complete this harmonious evocation of antiquity.

Described at the time as both neo-Greek and neo-Byzantine, the furnishings designed by the cabinetmaker Charles-Guillaume Diehl, with the aid of the dec-

Pierre-Eugène-Emile Hébert
1828-1893
The Servant firm
Factory of artistic bronzes in Paris
Neo-Greek Style Table
Designed before 1878
Ebony and wood varnished black, patinated gilt bronze, marble
Saint-Jean Fleuri
80 x 109 x 72.5 cm
Acquired with support from the Société des Amis du Musée d'Orsay

Charles-Guillaume Diehl
Cabinetmaker
1811-vers 1885
Jean Brandely
Draughtsman
Emmanuel Fremiet
Sculptor
1824-1910

Medallion Cabinet
1867
Cedar, walnut, ebony and
ivory, silvered bronze and
copper
238 x 151 x 60 cm
Purchased in 1973

orators Jean Brandely and the sculptors Gustave Fremiet and Emile Guillemin, were the most original pieces of Parisian cabinetmaking at the 1867 World's Fair; the decorative motifs of the huge *Medallion Cabinet* (1867) were inspired by the Merovingian chapter of French history, which provided Fremiet with the occasion to work on his favourite subjects: animals and soldiers.

One of the most beautiful examples of interior decoration at the height of the Second Empire is the splendid mansion of Marquise de Paiva, at 25 Avenue des Champs-Elysées, which was built and furnished from 1856 to 1866, by the architect Pierre Manguin. He surrounded himself with the most distinguished artists of the time, such as the painter Paul Baudry, and the sculptors Jean-Paul Aubé, Félix Barrias, Carrier-Belleuse, and Jules Dalou. These artists reinterpret with stunning panache an ornamental and allegorical repertoire mainly taken from the French Renaissance. The large drawing room, the main room for receiving guests with five tall windows overlooking the Champs-Elysées, featured, in addition to a ceiling painted by Baudry, a majestic fireplace and an elaborate mural decoration accentuated by four consoles. Dispersed between 1902 and 1904, two of the consoles are conserved at the Musée des Arts Décoratifs in Paris and at the Toledo Museum of Art; a third remains in private hands, and the fourth is now in the collection of the Musée d'Orsay. Entirely made of marble and bronze, these console tables were unique works of art that played an important role in the architect's choice of decor; they drew their inspiration from seventeenth-century Italian furniture, and the flowing, elegant style of Carrier-Belleuse bestowed them with refinement and sensuality.

Jules Desfossé, another figure concerned with promoting a union of the Fine Arts and Industry, brought in painters like Thomas Couture and Edouard Muller, to design his most outstanding wallpapers. The *Garden of Armida* (1854), the central part of a decor by Muller, made its mark as one of the masterpieces of the naturalist movement present in all of the decorative arts and which went across the diverse trends of eclecticism.

In reaction to the dehumanizing effects of mechanization, and refusing to collaborate with industrialists, a group of artists sought to regain the humanist artisan-artist ideal of the Renaissance. Charles-Jean Avisseau rediscovered the technical processes of Bernard Palissy and sparked a revival of artistic ceramic pieces. Counter to the processes of division of labour, Avisseau modelled, painted, baked, and sold his pieces himself. Similarly, Claudius Popelin returned to the tradition of sixteenth-century Limousin enamel work; his painted enamels clearly demonstrate this erudite spirit enthusiastic for the nation's past, which captivated both artists and amateurs of the time.

A source of fantasy and escape, the East, too, breathed new life into the fields of artisanal glassmaking and earthenware. Joseph Brocard and Théodore Deck discovered new possibilities for artistic expression in the decorative forms and techniques of Islam. In an attempt to rival the ancient lamps of Syrian and Egyptian mosques, Brocard renewed the popularity of blown and enamelled glass. The manufacturer Jules Vieillard made an original and ambitious earthenware and enamel version of an enamelled bottle, attributed to a fourteenth-century Egyptian or Syrian workshop and now conserved at the Musée du Louvre; it mixes elements from Adalbert de Beaumont's compendium of ornaments, Arab-Andalousian dishes in damascened copper, friezes and floral rinceaux reproducing Ottoman motifs. Deck

Albert-Ernest Carrier-Belleuse
1824-1887
in collaboration with
Aimé-Jules Dalou
1838-1902

under the direction of
Pierre Manguin
1815-1869
Console from the Paiva Mansion drawing room

1864-1865
gilt and patinated bronze, red marble, onyx, and alabaster
110 x 161 x 58 cm
Acquired by inheritor's donation in 1997

Charles-Jean Avisseau
1796-1871
Octave Guillaume de Rochebrune
?-1900
Cup and basin
1855
Fine earthenware with moulded and additive polychrome decorative motif
Cup: 34.5 x 26.5 cm
Basin: 8 x 51.5 cm
Purchased in 1983

J. Vieillard and Co.
Manufacturer of earthenware in Bordeaux, 1845-1895
Vase-Bottle and Dish
Circa 1878
Earthenware decorated with raised enamel; motif probably designed by Amédée de Caranza
Vase: 57 x 31 cm
Dish: D. 41 cm
Gift of Mr Robert Tschoudjouney, 1999

Emile-Auguste Reiber
1826-1893
Théodore Deck
1823-1891
Hanging Vase
Circa 1863
Earthenware, decorative pattern imprinted under turquoise-blue glazing
34 x 30.6 cm
Purchased in 1990

Emile–Auguste Reiber
1826-1893
Christofle and Co.
Jardinière
Designed in 1878
Partially gilt, silvered,
patinated in black on
ground patinated in red,
bronze patinated with
gold highlights, painted
tin.
13 x 32 x 25.6 cm
Purchased in 1985

Christofle et Cie
*Tray with natural
engraving*
Circa 1886
Silver-plated metal
11 x 46 cm
Purchased in 1989

succeeded in perfectly imitating the bright enamels of Turkish earthenware from Iznik, one of the most beautiful examples of which is the "Arabian" hanging vase, which he did in collaboration Emile Reiber and which attracted attention at the 1867 World's Fair in Paris and in London in 1871. In Deck's work, Chinese influences or, more rarely, the neo-Assyrian style were juxtaposed with the fourteenth-century decorative repertoire. Constant Sévin created for Barbedienne a range of Eastern-inspired enamel ornaments designed for industrial manufacture.

Japan, however, was soon to become the most influential country in the arts. The interest of Parisian collectors was aroused by the Chinese museum that Empress Eugénie had created, in 1863 at Fontainebleau, with objects plundered during the sacking of the Summer Palace and with gifts from the ambassadors of Siam. However, it was mainly the 1867 World's Fair that made Japan known to the Western public. Barbedienne and Christofle's first attempts at manufacturing cloisonné pieces dates from this period. For Christofle, Emile Reiber, who had become director of the design studios in 1865, created an artistic collection of ornaments that boldly rivalled the work of foundry casters and enamellers in China, Japan, the Indies, and Persia. Elaborated since 1869, the "Japanese clock" and its pair of candelabra look to Japan, China, and India, for both its decorative motif and technique; it is an adaptation of miniature Chinese screens, Indian elephant motifs, and enamelled panels Japanese in spirit. With their cast iron and perfect chasing, their red and black finishes, and gold and silver inlays, these cloisonnés are a distant interpretation of Eastern designs. At the 1878 World's Fair, Christofle presented a galvanic copper jardinière inlaid with flowers composed of silver petals and golden stamens. Its legs and handles are made of patinated bronze pinecones, highlighted with gold. These objects were produced in different colours on either a black or a brick red background. Later, the company inaugurated, in 1880, a series of metal objects whose leaf and flower motif was directly imprinted on them. One of the most remarkable examples of the emergence of Japanism in the decorative arts

Eugène Rousseau
1827-1890
Vase
Circa 1878
Glass, engraved and
painted pattern, plating
25 x 18 cm
Purchased in 1984

Lebeuf Millet and Co.
Creil and Montereau
Félix Bracquemond
1833-1914
Eugène Rousseau
1827-1890

Serving Dish for Fish
1867
Fine earthenware,
decorative motif
imprinted and painted
under glazing
69.4 x 27 cm
Purchased in 1983

is a fine earthenware dinner service containing over two hundred pieces, commissioned in 1867 to the painter-printmaker Félix Bracquemond by the artist and shopkeeper Eugène Rousseau, who himself created glass works of similar inspiration. Bracquemond selected his decorative motifs from Japanese prints and illustrated books and it looks as though he haphazardly threw them onto the white ground of the earthenware. The spread of this Oriental trend to furniture, however, was slower. Examples include the cabinet by Duvinage (circa 1877-1878), which features ivory and exotic wood inlays and is compartmentalized and accentuated by flower and insect motifs, and the wardrobe designed by Edouard Detaille, which incorporates a portrait of a Japanese warrior. Both offer a very free transposition of elements borrowed from a fanciful facet of the East.

Edouard Lièvre
1829-1886
Edouard Detaille
1848-1912

*Piece of furniture with
two parts: cupboard on
console table*
Circa 1877
Rosewood, chased and
gilt bronze, engraved iron
211 x 111 x 57 cm
Purchased in 1981

Edward Welby Pugin
1834-1875
Granville Chair
1870
Stained and varnished
oak, ebony, and bronze
81 x 51 x 51 cm
Purchased in 1984

In Great Britain, industrialization, which emerged in the second half of the eighteenth century, brought about a reaction against the dehumanizing effects of the assembly line. A theoretical reaction was led by John Ruskin, who challenged industrial work and dreamed of regaining the Middle Ages; whereas a conciliatory and pragmatic reaction was headed by Henry Cole, the organizer of the first World's Fair in 1851, in London, and instigator of reforms striving for an alliance between art and industry.

The true originator of this movement is the architect Augustus Welby Pugin, who conceived a notion of architecture that would result from a tight union between art, craftsmanship, and technology. Promoter of the return to Gothicism, he moved little by little toward a rational art, in an approach similar to that of Viollet-le-Duc. Pugin designed furniture with simple, very constructed forms, leaving visible the means of assembly, that is, the mortice and tenon joints and pegs. After his death, his son Edward Welby Pugin took over the family firm and picked up the designs where his father had left off. The role of architects is primordial in the aesthetic of the Arts and Crafts movement: Pugin, Philip Webb, William Burges, Arthur Mackmurdo, Edward Godwin, Ernest Gimson, and Charles Voysey, all were looking for a total art, and considered it a necessity that everyday life should be beautiful and that all must be given the same close attention: wallpapers, printed or woven textiles, furniture painted or in natural wood, ceramics (earthenware and stoneware were preferred over porcelain), practical utensils in copper, glass...

William Morris, who created in 1861 Morris and Company, was the only one who found a way to reconcile the reassertion of the value of craftsmanship with industrial distribution. First a painter closed tied to Pre-Raphaelites such as Rossetti and Burne-Jones (who collaborated on some of his works), Morris worked in perfect harmony with the architect Philip Webb; the latter had built, in 1859, the Masion Rouge for Morris, who furnished it himself entirely. The *Buffet* designed around 1880 by Webb and Morris revealed their attraction to furniture of medieval inspiration, to rather heavy forms in solid wood, and to polychrome ornamentation. For Count de Carlisle, Morris designed an interior that placed a frieze painted by Burne-Jones, depicting the story of Psyche, within his floral, naturalist furnishings. These same plant and flower patterns were multiplied through their reproduction on fabrics and wallpapers and were to become the work for which he is best known. Soliciting the craft of William de Morgan, William Morris trans-

Philip Webb,
architect
1831-1915
Morris and Company,
London and Merton
Abbey
Buffet
Circa 1880

Black-varnished
mahogany, partially
painted and gilt, painted
and varnished leather
repoussé
204 x 202 x 63 cm
Purchased in 1979

Philip Webb
1831-1915
Morris, Marshall, Faulkner
and Company
Worktable
Circa 1860-1868
Oak, brass
73 x 167 x 61 cm
Purchased in 1979

William Morris
Designer
1834-1896
William de Morgan
Ceramist
1839-1917
Decorative Wall Tiles
Prototype designed circa
1876
Tiles of enamelled
earthenware
163.5 x 905 cm
Gift of Soviété des Amis
du Musée d'Orsay, 1989

posed them to bright enamelled earthenware panels for the walls of the Membland Hall, circa 1876-1877.

On the encouragement of Burne-Jones and Morris, the architect and designer Henri Benson opened a first factory in 1880. He produced many light fixtures with pared down forms, often made in brass and varnished copper.

The main contradiction of the Arts and Crafts movement resided in the desire to impart beauty to all objects, while most often favouring the rebirth of very expensive craftsmanship only within the reach of a rich clientele. Following Morris's example, many artists formed craft guilds that were often ephemeral since they were not profitable owing to their refusal to implement industrial techniques. A. H. Mackmurdo, one of the most original figures of the movement, founded the Century Guild in 1882, together with William de Morgan, Selwyn Image, and Voysey. In 1886, Century Guild made an impact at the World's Fair in Liverpool; Mackmurdo presented a prototype of a chair with a high back and ledge, as well as a cabinet whose pared down form displayed Japanese influence. William de Morgan rediscovered the techniques of Islam and, above all, of Persia, in his flamboyant earthenware pieces with a metallic lustre. Over almost fifty years, Voysey designed motifs for wallpapers and textiles, adroitly combining stylization with natural forms in his wool draperies *(Drapery,* 1896).

Thomas Jeckyll, Edward-William Godwin, and Christopher Dresser put themselves at the service of industry; the discovery of Japanese decorative art allowed them to introduce light, angular, spare shapes. Godwin analyzed the art of Japanese carpenters and, in his Anglo-Japanese furniture, he underscored its structure and construction, full and empty spaces, and light and shadow, through the use of broken or interrupted lines. For the third count of Limerick, he built and furnished a neo-Gothic castle, whose furniture was dispersed sometime around 1949. He bestowed Gothic Revival with a pared down version, better adapted to modern times, revivified by Japan, and composed of frankness and simplicity: natural wood grains and nickel-plated brass accents were the only ornamentation of a strictly geometric shape.

The Worcester Royal Porcelain Company, which enjoyed brilliant success at World Fairs, showed its admiration for the East, by mixing Persian, Indian, and Sino-Japanese sources. Richard William Binns, who exclusively directed the factory from 1862 on, could also demonstrate a radical attitude, as can be seen in the tea set tray, printed with abstract, monochrome discs in the spirit of patterns published by Thomas Cutler at the time, in his famous *Grammar of Japanese Ornaments,* as well as the Anglo-Japanese style developed by Godwin.

Dresser founded his design agency in 1862, and his prototypes were reproduced by some fifty first-rate manufacturers, in the most diverse materials and techniques possible. A professor of botany and an influential theoretician, he published treatises on *The Art of Decorative Design* (1862), *The Principles of Decorative Design* (1873), and *Modern Ornamentation* (1866). He stylized ornamentation by making it geometric. In 1876-1877, he was one of the first Western decorators to travel to Japan, with a view to discovering all the aspects of the life and craft of Japanese art. Surprisingly modern, his silverware designs reveal the artist's evolution toward a rigorous art through his exploitation of purity of form (*Soup Tureen*, 1880; *Sauceboat*, 1880).

William Arthur Smith Benson
Pair of Candlesticks
Prototype designed before 1887
Silver-plated bronze
11.5 x 35 x 17 cm
Purchased in 1991

Edward William Godwin
1833-1886
William Watt
Furniture manufacturer, London
Dressing Table
1870

Deal, nickel-plated metal, and glass
187 x 150 x 48 cm
Gift of Société des Amis du Musée d'Orsay, 1995

Christopher Dresser
1834-1904
The Herkin and Heath firm, Birmingham
Soup Tureen
Model patented in 1880
Silver-plated metal and ebony
21 x 31 x 23.5 cm
Purchased in 1985

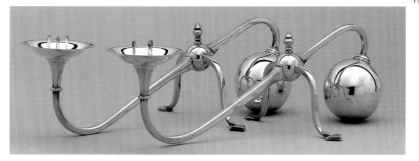

"What we were feeling about 1894 can best be compared to the sense of deliverance we feel at the first signs of spring." This revival, as expressed by Henry Van de Velde, one of the architects who founded the "new style", summed up the wave of experimentation and the thirst for original forms of expression in architecture and decoration that had been in evidence in Europe since the 1880s. The idea of total art, the fruit of collaboration between artists in all techniques, that had been rationalised by Viollet le Duc in *Entretiens sur l'architecture* (1873), was the legacy of the Arts and Crafts movement in England. The movement was supported and publicised by the large number of reviews that flowered at the time, exhibited its creations in avant-garde salons and soon took on an international character, spreading to the main European capitals. In Paris in 1895, the opening of Siegfried Bing's gallery *L'Art nouveau* officially established the existence of a style.

In 1892, the architect and decorator Victor Horta crystallised the new ideas in building the Tassel house in Brussels. The same search for unity and harmony guided the decoration of the house he built in 1899-1904 for the industrialist Octave Aubecq, but the style was less radical. The arching ridges of the woodwork, the stems that emphasised the framework of French doors and furniture, became more stylised; the overall impression was more austere and the structures emerged more clearly. Paul Hankar, one of the most brilliant creators in the Belgian Art Nouveau movement, along with Horta and Van de Velde, preferred planes, graphics and a restrained approach to exalt the structure of his buildings and his furniture. This can be seen in the *Double door for the Studio of the Artist Ciamberlani* in Brussels, 1897, and in his dining table with its column legs and grid-shaped stretcher.

Gustave Serurier-Bovy crafted his furniture in a coherent, rigorous manner; he toned down his taste for inflections and curves, which he framed in straighter lines, adding abstract patterns to enhance the natural beauty of the wood (*Dressing Table*, 1899).

Victor Horta
1861-1947
Chair
Designed circa 1902-1904
for the dining room of
the Aubecq house, built in
Brussels in 1899-1904
(demolished in 1950)
Moulded ash
97 x 171.5 x 69.5 cm
Purchased in 1980

Paul Hankar
1859-1901
Dining Room Table
For the dining room of
the Ciamberlani house,
Brussels, built in 1897-1898
Moulded oak and mahogany
78 x 190 x 110 cm
Gift from Hokkaido
Shimbun, 1998

Gustave Serrurier-Bovy
1858-1910
Dressing Table
Designed in 1899
Waxed, moulded, brass
188 x 137 x 57 cm
Purchased in 1984

Henry van de Velde's creations referred to the same handcrafted tradition. In 1893, he abandoned painting and built and decorated his own home, Bloemenwerf house in the Uccle suburb of Brussels. Refusing anything artificial and super-fluous, he designed a chair with pure, dynamic lines; it was industrialised and its success help spread the new approach throughout Europe. Similarly, the armchair he designed for the banker Biart in 1896 was soon to be found in many Belgian or German homes. Van de Velde achieved perfection in his desire to combine form and decoration with his large *Desk:* the abstract, dynamic lines create a continuous, lively rhythm and ornamentation is restricted to the highly functional bronze-gilt mouldings and handles.

Belgium produced other astonishing creations in the decorative arts. Léopold van Strydonck, jeweller to the Belgian court, exhibited an extraordinary arrange-ment in the Congo Pavilion at Tervuren during the International Exhibition in Brussels in 1897. The interior design of the pavilion had been entrusted to Hankar; Strydonck's exhibit was "The Struggle of Good and Evil" arranged around one of the elephant tusks brought from the Congo and made available to the artists by King Leopold II. Van Strydonck left the tusk unadorned and contrasted it with a furious tangle of bronze snakes...

In Amsterdam, about 1895-1898, Hendrik Petrus Berlage followed the lead of British artists such as A.W.N. Pugin, in designing a chair in which the construction was clearly apparent. Michel De Klerck, one of the foremost architects in the Amsterdam School, designed a thirteen-piece set of furniture for a dining room and a drawing room. A combination of triangular, trapezoidal and parabolic pieces countered the stability of the base. Aggressive decorative elements, teeth and claws, no doubt inspired by the "primitive" arts, gave the furniture a disconcerting, hostile feeling.

Henry van de Velde
1863-1957
Writing Desk
Designed in 1898-1899
Oak, gilt-bronze, copper,
leather
128 x 268 x 122 cm
Purchased in 1987, thanks
to the Crédit Lyonnais

Léopold van Strydonck
1861-1937
*"The Struggle of Good
and Evil" – Mounted
Elephant Tusk*
1897
Ivory, bronze
76 x 70 x 35 cm
Purchased in 1989

Hendrik Petrus Berlage
1856-1934
Chair
Designed circa 1895-1898
Oak
94 x 44 x 56 cm
Purchased in 1987

Richard Riemerschmid
1868-1957
Vereinigte Werkstätten für
Kunst und Handwerk,
Munich
Pair of Candlesticks
Designed in 1897
Brass
35.6 x 16 cm
Purchased in 2002

The German Richard Riemerschmid designed furniture intended for mass production, using sturdy, cheap materials and eschewing all decoration; but this venture was a failure (*Chair,* model designed in 1902). He took part in the Jungendstil movement and in 1898, with Peter Behrens, Bruno Paul and Bernhard Pankok, he formed the Vereinigte Werkstätten für Kunst und Handwerk (United Studios for Arts and Crafts); he was also one of the founders of the Deutscher Werkbund, in 1907, the first real attempt to combine art and industry. The Musée d'Orsay has one of Riemerschmid's finest and most innovative designs, a pair of sober, fluid candlesticks designed in 1897. Bruno Paul's *Armchair,* which was part of a set shown at the Universal Exhibition in Paris in 1900, is constructed from smooth planes with no relief or modelling, yet a touch of humour counters its rigorous design, because the armrests end in clenched fists! The success of the art and craft studios was shown by the opening of branches in Hamburg, Bremen and Berlin, and by designs from foreign artists such as the Dutchman Eisenlöffel, who produced metal household objects of a stylistic purity that aroused Van de Velde's admiration.

Peter Behrens shared the dream of Ernst Ludwig, Grand Duke of Hesse, to create an artists'colony at Darmstadt; the Viennese architect Joseph Maria Olbrich was put in charge of the colony, with directions to build a "modern quarter" as a forerunner of a new type of housing. Behrens built and equipped one of the colony's seven houses; the dining room chairs, made of white painted poplar, are remarkable for their bold design, the outward movement of the feet, and their rigorous construction balanced by the curve of the armrests and legs.

Northern European countries sought to create a national art deeply rooted in their heritage: in Norway, Johan Borgersen and Lars Kinsarvik worked with simple forms, carving abstract patterns, dynamic curves suggesting waves, ropes, sea monsters or even creatures from Norse legends such as witches and dragons. Kinsarvik underlined their power with bright greens and yellows and touches of red and blue (*Armchair,* circa 1900).

In Russia, national romanticism found an outlet in the creations of the Talachkino studios established by Princess Marie Tenicheva in the outskirts of Smolensk. The furniture, household objects, sleds, and balalaikas they put out, followed by textiles, ceramics, and enamelled copper objects in austere shapes with a primitive tinge, were so popular that Talachkino was represented at the Paris Exhibition in 1900 (*Chairs,* circa 1900).

The Polish sculptor and painter Boleslas Biegas produced spare, symbolist cartoons for wall hangings, seeking to conserve and reinvigorate Poland's country crafts, but with overtones of the aesthetics of the Vienna Sezession.

Bruno Paul
1874-1968
Vereinigte Werkstätten
für Kunst und Handwerk,
Munich
Armchair
Model shown at the
Universal Exhibition, Paris,
1900
Elm
85.5 x 71 x 66 cm
Purchased with
the contribution of
the Société des Amis
du Musée d'Orsay, 1999

Peter Behrens
1868-1940
J.D. Heyman Factory,
Hamburg
Chair
Designed in 1901 for the
artist's house in Darmstadt
White painted poplar, red
leather upholstery
106 x 65 x 45.4 cm
Purchased with
the contribution of
the Société des Amis
du Musée d'Orsay, 1999

Lars Kinsarvick
1846-1925
Armchair
Carved, painted wood
95 x 49.5 x 55 cm
Purchased in 2003

Italy and Spain:
Carlo Bugatti, Antoni Gaudí

Carlo Bugatti
1856-1940
Chair
1902
Wood covered with
parchment, painted
highlights and embossed
copper
97 x 37.2 x 53 cm
Purchased in 1992

In Milan, from 1880, Carlo Bugatti directed a factory producing artistic furniture which quickly won international renown. In 1902 he displayed four wildly original sets of furniture at the Turin Decorative Arts Exhibition, including a Games and Conversation Room based on the morphology of a snail; this wooden *Chair* covered with parchment and painted highlights was part of the set. The chair is animated by a dynamic, flowing, supple movement which achieves perfect fusion of structure and decoration in a completely new form.

The Lombard artist Alessandro Mazzucotelli took a very pared down, stylised approach to a wrought iron light fitting decorated with a dragonfly, a motif which became a favourite with Art Nouveau artists (*Electric Light Fitting*, circa 1903-1906).

Architecture took a sumptuous turn in Barcelona: on the occasion of the Universal Exhibition which was held there in 1888, the medieval quarter turned itself into a modern city stretching from the sea to the mountain. Three architects dominated construction in this period: Josef Puig i Cadafalch, Lluís Domènech i Montaner and, soaring above them all, Antoni Gaudí. In 2001, the Musée d'Orsay was enriched by a superb set of works by Gaudí, evoking his most important creations, which were designed as total art works; like Guimard in France, Gaudí brought about a total fusion of architecture and decoration, which he imagined in a dynamic, organic way, rejecting symmetry and straight lines. The wrought iron *Flower Stand* comes from Palacio Güell; the extraordinary corner *Display Case* from the dining room of the Casa Battló (1904-1906), a unique piece built into the woodwork, recalling the design of the façade and the house's curving interior and exterior decoration. The concrete flower stand incrusted with fragments of coloured glass, pottery and porcelain, which also comes from the Casa Battló, reminds us of the expressive polychromy of the facade and anticipates the famous trencadis bench in Güell Park. Lastly, the gilt wood console table and the astonishing quivering aquatic mirrors come from Gaudí's last large secular architectural project, the Casa Milà (1905-1910); it was the culmination of his dream of sculpture-architecture, a sort of stone cliff rippling like the sea, carved by the wind, worn away by erosion.

The purchase of these outstanding works was subsidised by the Heritage Fund and private sponsorship. Some major pieces, the two mirrors, and a set of paving stones from the Casa Milà, were generously donated by Pedro and Kiki Uhart, along with a drawing room chair by the cabinetmaker who best represents Catalan Modernism, Joan Busquets i Jané.

In 1888, Paco Durrio, from Valladolid, obtained a bursary to study sculpture in Paris; he soon made his mark in the colony of Spanish artists, most of whom were from Catalonia: Santiago Rusinol, Joaquin Sunyer, Isido Nonell, Pablo Picasso and Juan Gris. The human figure played a core role in his work and his closed, wild, sometimes deformed faces are strongly reminiscent of Paul Gauguin's ceramics. Durrio had met Gauguin after his first trip to Tahiti, sometime between 1893 and 1895 and he is known to have owned some of the French artist's work (*Anthropomorphic Pot*, circa 1905-1906).

Antoni Gaudí
1852-1926
Three-legged Triangular Jardiniere
From the Casa Battló (1904-1906), Madrid
Concrete inset with a circular mirror and fragments of coloured glass, faience, porcelain decorated with floral motifs and gilt porcelain.
22 x 21 cm
Purchased with the help of the Heritage Fund and sponsorship coordinated by Nikkei newspaper, 2001

Antoni Gaudí
1852-1926
Corner Display Case
From the dining room in the Casa Battló (1904-1906), Madrid
Moulded oak, bevelled panes
232 x 82 x 63 cm
Purchased with the help of the Heritage Fund and sponsorship coordinated by Nikkei newspaper, 2001

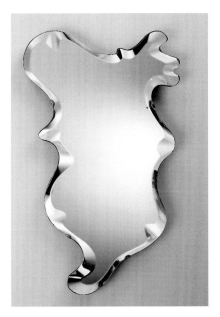

Antoni Gaudí
1852-1926
Wall Mirror
From the Casa Milà (1905-1910), Barcelona
Bevelled mirror over a wooden core
52 x 31 x 3 cm
Gift from Pedro and Kiki Uhart, 2001

Paco Durrio
1868-1940
Anthropomorphic Pot
Circa 1905-1906
Glazed stoneware
37.8 x 23.5 cm
Purchased in 1996

As a self-styled "artistic architect", Hector Guimard pursued the same utilitarian ideal as Victor Horta, whose Tassel house he had seen in Brussels in 1894. At the time he was building a block of flats at 16, rue de La Fontaine, in Paris, known as Castel Béranger, which he modified on his return from Belgium. The facade of this building won a prize awarded by the City of Paris in 1898. The vocabulary of the "Guimard style", a term which appeared for the first time in 1903, shows a preference for asymmetry, arabesques and long plant-like curves which invaded his approach to all kinds of materials: wood, mosaic, ceramics, wrought iron, stained glass and wallpaper.

For the billiard room and the small drawing room in the Roy house in Les Gévrils (Loiret), he used models he had designed for Castel Béranger. *The Mantelpiece, Smoking Room Bench, Chest Seat and Stained Glass Window* pulse with rhythms borrowed from the plant kingdom, the vital principle of the stem; all impulse points are emphasised by knots of abstract motifs. The early twentieth century brought a change in Guimard's style, as is shown by the *Armchair* designed for Castel Val at Chaponval, built in 1902-1903; rather than lines, he concentrated on contrasting solids and voids, using the curve of the seat, back and arms to emphasise the function of the chair and relegating abstract decoration to the ends of the armrests.

The architect designed a series of iron ornaments for city buildings and suburban villas and had them cast by the Saint Dizier foundries, about 1903-1905. But the attempt to market these ornaments for buildings, gardens or cemeteries failed because his designs were so individual that they were difficult to fit into an environment that had not been designed by Guimard himself.

Hector Guimard
1867-1942
Armchair
1903
Pear wood, original
repoussé and tooled
leather upholstery
106 x 76 x 56 cm
Purchased in 1989

Hector Guimard
1867-1942
Le Cœur et Cie, carpen-
ters, Paris
Smoking Room Couch
From the estate of the
pharmacist Albert Roy at

Les Gévrils (Loiret), 1897
Moulded, carved jarrah,
tooled metal
260 x 262 x 60 cm
Purchased in 1979

Jewellery offered Art Nouveau a vast field to explore. René Lalique combined the subtle palette of precious stones, cloisonné or engraved enamel, with horn, ivory and glass in his naturalistic and symbolist jewellery. Hispanic and Japanese influences, as well as the fashion for chignons brought combs and hairpins to the fore. Hair was an overwhelmingly important part of Art Nouveau's ideal woman and had to be beautifully dressed. Lalique chose the umbel as a symbol, stylising the fine stems rising into a mass of white flowers, and used pale horn, gold and diamonds to create it. Lucien Gaillard combined horn and opals, or again horn, gold, mother-of-pearl and diamonds to translate fragile may blossoms and leaves just before they wilt. No doubt encouraged by the success enjoyed by Emile Gallé, Lalique set up a glass workshop in 1898. Inspired by plants and sea creatures, the *Scent Bottle* also refers to eighteenth century designs. Henri Vever worked in partnership with Eugène Grasset, who designed "Merovingian" jewellery for him. The *Apparitions* brooch with its Symbolist themes shows two masks emerging from a cloudy or watery mass; it uses enamel, gold, ivory and topaz cabochons. Fernand Thesmar designed colourful, transparent enamel cloisonné with gold, sometimes applied over soft-paste porcelain. The sculptor, goldsmith and enameller Eugène Feuillâtre obtained original effects by laying translucent enamel over silver (*Vase with a Lake Landscape*, 1903-1904). Armand Point revived a workshop at Haute-Claire in the spirit of the guilds of olden times and worked with a team producing enamel, pottery and embroidery. Georges Bastard made luxury products from the animal materials favoured by Art Nouveau designers: mother-of-pearl, horn, tortoise-shell, and ivory which were skilfully carved and worked in open designs.

René Lalique
1860-1945
"Cow Parsnip" Hairpins
Circa 1902-1903
Carved horn, chased gold
and diamonds
21.5 x 8.5 cm
Purchased in 1995

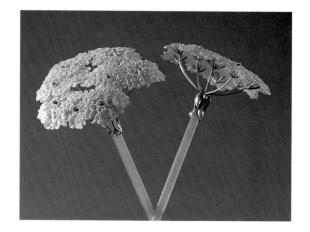

René Lalique
1860-1945
Scent Bottle
Circa 1900-1902
Blown glass, lost wax
moulded glass, molten
and chased gold
10.5 cm
Purchased in 1988

Georges Bastard
1881-1939
"Barley Ears" Fan
1911
Horn and mother-of-pearl
21.4 x 38.7 cm
Purchased in 1912

Eugène Grasset
1845-1917
Vever
Jeweller, Paris
"Apparitions" Brooch
1900

Repoussé gold,
translucent and opaque
cloisonné enamel, ivory,
topaz
6.2 x 3.9 cm
Purchased at the 1900
Universal Exhibition

Eugène Feuillâtre
1870-1916
Sweet Box
Circa 1903-1904
Silver, enamel and crystal
8.3 x 14.5 cm
Purchased in 1904

Ceramics played a leading role in the renaissance of the applied arts; in the 1870s, potters began a searching analysis of the processes they used, renewing the very idea of ceramics. Ernest Chaplet was the first in this brilliant school of modern potters; excited by the quality of ceramic work from the Far East, he worked on stoneware and glazed porcelain, which he coated with brilliant reds and blues. He then developed a range of glazed stoneware, decorated with highly stylised, cloisonné motifs, outlined with gold, which floated along the surface of the vase without ever repeating themselves. Chrysanthemums and water lilies flowered freely over the vase in the Japanese manner. Alexandre Bigot also drew inspiration from China and Japan. His rustic creations were decorated with matt yellow, blue-green and brown glazes. Towards 1900, he produced tiles and relief stonework for architectural decoration, and interpreted designs by sculptors and architects (Charpentier, Guimard).

Auguste Delaherche was one of the leading figures in French ceramic art and the Musée d'Orsay's collection has been enriched by a number of rare pieces purchased directly from the potter's workshop or donated by Mrs René Bureau, along with the artist's archives and all his drawings. This enables us to trace the development of his style which led him, about 1900, to concentrate solely on the beauty of the material itself, and the gleam or depth of the glaze. More stylised forms and plain, matt colours gradually won over gloss and glazes (*"Cabbage Leaf" Vase*, 1892; *Large Vase*, 1893).

The Danish artist Niels Hansen Jacobsen hand-finished his earthenware creations to modify the shape or give the handle the gnarled look of a branch. (*Pot*, 1903) The Royal Copenhagen Porcelain Manufactory drew on folklore and popular themes of dancers and musicians to produce simply shaped objects, in which the dazzling white glazed porcelain forms not only the background, but becomes the colour of snow-covered trees and ice crystals, giving the vases a fresh look. The Swedish manufactory at Rørstrand, directed by the graphic artist Alf Wallander, used marine motifs such as slightly raised pink and violet porcelain fish and octopuses on a greyish or greenish white ground and was soon rivalling the Copenhagen manufactory.

Ernest Chaplet
1835-1909
Flower Pot Holder
Circa 1885-1887
Glazed stoneware, porcelain slip, gold highlights
26 x D. 33 cm
Gift from the Friends of the Musée d'Orsay, 1995

Auguste Delaherche
1857-1940
Vase
1893
Glazed stoneware
51.2 cm
Gift from Mrs Christiane
Hillemand, 2003

Richard Bocher
decorator
Royal Copenhagen
Porcelain Manufactory
Vase
1919
Porcelain
46 cm
Purchased in 1991

Rørstrand Manufactory
Octopus Vase
1900
Porcelain
24 x 10.7 cm
Purchased in 1998

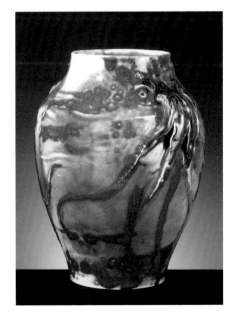

In the closing decade of the nineteenth century, the town of Nancy enjoyed a flurry of artistic activity: in 1901, the Nancy school officially received its statutes as a "Provincial Alliance of Artistic Industries". In this flourishing city, a group of manufacturers and craftsmen headed by Emile Gallé proclaimed the principle of the "unity of art". They regarded nature as the sole, inexhaustible source of renewal for the decorative arts and insisted on the duty to teach others to reinvigorate a highly skilled labour force.

In 1901, François Vaxelaire established a drapery and fancy goods store in the rue Raugraff in Nancy; he asked the architects Charles and Emile André to design the building. Emile André worked on the interior design in association with Eugène Vallin, a carpenter, cabinetmaker and sculptor. They gave pride of place to wood carved into plant forms and dotted with clematis flowers, and stained glass windows designed by André and executed by Jacques Gruber.

The decorator and cabinetmaker Louis Majorelle teamed carved mahogany with naturalistic inlaid work, adapting the dynamic lines of the decoration to the curves of the furniture. He adorned the corners of some pieces with gilt-bronze water lilies or stylised orchids, which accentuated the construction of the furniture and strengthened its balance and stability. Light fittings designed by Majorelle were executed in collaboration with Daum and belong to the "Lotus" and "Water Lilies" series dating from 1902.

Stained glass played a major role in the renewal of interior decoration and architects called on well-known artists to design it. Albert Besnard, a painter and decorator, put all his skill as a colourist into the stained glass panels depicting *Swans on Lake Annecy,* for the French doors made by Henri Carot. After a trip to the United States in 1894, the art dealer Siegfried Bing decided to promote Art Nouveau in his famous Paris gallery; he commissioned ten stained glass windows from the American Louis Comfort Tiffany after cartoons by the Nabi painters Bonnard, Denis, Vallotton, Vuillard and Toulouse-Lautrec (*At the New Circus*).

Henri de Toulouse-Lautrec
1864-1901
and **Louis Comfort Tiffany**
1848-1933
At the New Circus, 1895
"American" mottled and rippled glass, cabochons
120 x 85 cm
Gift from Henri Dauberville, in the name of his children, Béatrice and Guy-Patrice, 1979

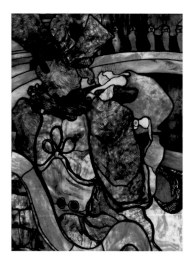

Emile André
1880-1944
Eugène Vallin
1856-1922
Jacques Gruber
1870-1930

*Door (fitting room for
François Vaxelaire stores),*
1901
Mahogany, "American"
rippled glass, opalescent
glass, copper
198 x 182 x 65 cm
Purchased in 1983

Louis Majorelle
1859-1926
"Orchid" Desk
Circa 1905-1909
Mahogany, letterwood,
gilt bronze, embossed
leather
95 x 145 x 70 cm
Purchased in 1980

Emile Gallé
1846-1904
"Mysterious Grapes" Flask
Double layer of blown
glass, metal inclusions
(gold and platinum), hot
application of cabochons,
etched decoration;
opalescent blown glass
stopper; carved, stained
pear-tree wood base.
40 x 12.5 cm
Gift from Mrs Jean
Bourgogne and her chil-
dren in memory of Jean
Bourgogne, grandson of
Emile Gallé, through the
Friends of the Musée
d'Orsay, 2000

New processes were being tried in glassmaking and enamelling. Commissioned by the Ministry of Fine Arts in 1892, the sculptor and ceramist Henri Cros designed a polychrome wall fountain in glass paste on the theme of the history of water, for the Musée du Luxembourg. The glassmaker and ceramist Albert Dammouse invented a process for producing very fine glass paste decorations, whereas François Décorchemeont preferred a more transparent, thicker glass paste.

Under the Second Empire, the great names in the crystal business suddenly proved to be very creative: Rousseau, Léveillé, the Pannier brothers at *L'escalier de cristal* experimented with new processes for colouring or eglomising glass. Outside France, eyes were riveted on the fragile corollas of the cups made by Koepping, who worked for the Royal Manufactory in Berlin; in New York, Louis Comfort Tiffany developed an opalescent material, in 1892, using a combination of several processes: irisation, filigree, gold and silver inclusions, and it became universally known under the trademark "Favrile glass".

Gallé inherited the family ceramic and glassmaking tradition; he continued to produce faience like his father Charles Gallé, but renewed its decoration with the shapes and colours of regional plants, which he studied as a keen botanist. His research led him to a dense, fine, sonorous paste which he decorated with flaw-less opaque glazes. Although he still used popular themes, he took inspiration from the East, especially China and Japan, for original creations such as this *Decorative Dish,* a Japanese interpretation of a work attributed to Bernard Palissy. He drew on Egyptian mythology for a *Jardiniere* in the shape of the falcon Horus, but nature was still his favourite model.

At first, glasswork stayed true to the Western tradition in terms of shape and to ancient sources in terms of decoration (*Ceremonial Glasses,* between 1867 and 1876). But from the mid 1870s, decoration taken directly from Japanese art began to appear, while Islamic and Persian traditions suggested new forms and techniques. The *Flower Holder* is an astonishing association of Japanese motifs, insects, flowers and grasses drawn in a light, linear style, and European landscapes; it combines the techniques of blown and crackle glass, and applications, with a painted, enam-elled and gilded decoration. The vase *Bindweed in October,* 1891, which has two layers of blown crystal, combines an etched décor and inclusions, while the *On Such a Night* cup is treated like a cameo, playing on three layers of crystal to obtain a range of blues, diffuse greens and black; it has inclusions of metal flecks and an etched decoration. Gallé mastered these processes perfectly; they became mes-sengers for his imagination which found in nature an endless source of poetic and musical "correspondences". *Bindweed in October* murmurs a line from Verlaine: "You gazed upon my melancholy", while *On Such a Night* conjures up a melodious night like the music from Berlioz's opera *The Trojans.* The *Onion Flowers* cornet made for Gallé's display at the Universal Exhibition of 1900 is a fine example of inlaid glass. Wildflowers and exotic blooms, insects, and sea creatures began to invade cups and vases. In 1889-1890, Gallé created a lidded pot for his friend the art critic Roger Marx; *Still Water* was the colour of moss and deep water with light yellowish-green bubbles. "Deep down there is a tangled burst of turquoise wings, raised or incised; vast wings of silver gauze, with pearly patches, the jut-ting eyes and tails of dragonflies, a fanciful beetle with long legs, striped wing sheaths and a deep azure sheen; water seeping from mica-flecked sands." Dazzled by nature's endless store of secrets, spurred on by the evocative power of Victor

Emile Gallé
1846-1904
Flower Holder
Designed circa 1878-1880
"Moonlight" glass, crackle glass with applications,

painted, enamelled and gilt decoration
Gilt-bronze mount
24 x 22 cm
Purchased in 1981

Emile Gallé
1846-1904
Hand with Seaweed and Shells
1904

Etched crystal with inclusions and applications
33.4 x 13.4 cm
Gift from the artist's descendents, 1990

Emile Gallé
1846-1904
"On Such a Night" Cup
1894
Blown glass in three layers, metallic fleck inclu-

sions, etched decoration, partly gilded
13.3 x 13.5 cm
Purchased in 1895

Hugo's poetry, snatches of which he engraved on his pieces, Gallé produced here one of his most inspired and poetic pieces. *Mysterious Grapes,* 1892, was a gift for his friend Count Robert de Montesquiou; he was influenced by Chinese objects in hard stone when designing the flask and used the colours and the composition to evoke the grapes ripening in the sun, then the liqueur pressed from them and lastly the evaporating spirits materialised by the opaline swirls of the stopper.

Gallé last glass creation was *Hand with Seaweed and Shells,* which uses the symbolism of underwater life, the "enamels and cameos of the sea". Suggestive of antique ex-votos, medieval reliquaries or oriental religions, the *Hand* is above all a mysterious, poetic "correspondence" with the world beneath the sea.

A longstanding interest in woodwork and a desire to see his ceramics and glasswork perfectly displayed prompted Gallé to produce "carved and inlaid woodwork" on an industrial scale. His production was divided into two categories: his "shelves and small pieces of furniture at a modest price" were well received, while his "deluxe furniture" drew some sharp criticism. Sold at prices which reflected the species of timber used and the degree of finishing, his chairs, sideboards, dessert trays and occasional tables were often designed in traditional styles and decorated in Gallé's naturalistic taste. Poppies lent their shapes to small columns, banisters, and console tables and decorated the inlay of a shelf, 1890-1892, or supported a table top (*Keep the Hearts you have Won,* 1895). *Winter Plants,* a showcase designed for the Universal Exhibition in 1889, was made to "contain the picture books which blossom around Christmas and New Year". The glass is etched with snowy landscapes and snowflakes and the drawers are adorned with holly and fir.

Emile Gallé's last creation, *The Display Case,* was commissioned in 1897 by the magistrate Henry Hirsch. The dragonflies, ubiquitous and usually so aerial in Gallé's art, are monolithic here and the unit is heavily monumental.

Emile Gallé
1846-1904
Display Case with Dragonflies
1904
Ironwood, fossil oak, bird's eye mahogany, pur-ple wood, mother-of-pearl inlay, patinated glass, hard stone, chased and patinated bronzes.
234 x 154 x 64.5 cm
Purchased in 1982

Jean Carriès
1855-1894
"The Frogman"
Circa 1891
Glazed stoneware
31.5 x 36 x 38 cm
Purchased in 1980

The principle of *artistic unity* which underpinned the aesthetic theories of the proponents of Art Nouveau was proclaimed in France with the official abolition of the distinction between "major" and "minor" arts; in 1891, the applied arts were admitted to the annual Salon of the Société Nationale des Beaux-Arts, alongside the fine arts of painting and sculpture.

Many sculptors made their contribution to the decorative arts: Alexandre Charpentier, Jean Baffier, Jean Dampt and Rupert Carabin, all sculptors converted to "decoration", were the forerunners of a revival of domestic arts and they explored the possibilities of a modern style that would be affordable and widely available. Jules Baffier created pewter tableware in plain designs, while Rodin's pupil Jules Desbois worked successfully with silver and pewter. Jean Carriès, acclaimed by critics and his contemporaries for his work as a sculptor, discovered Japanese ceramics at the Universal Exhibition of 1878, mastered the technique of stoneware and presented a highly successful display at the Société Nationale des Beaux-Arts in 1892. Gallé enthused: "You are young and brilliant! All by yourself you have discovered some marvellous secrets in our ancient trade." The State bought a number of glazed stoneware objects in unusual colours for the national collections; Carriès had also exhibited a number of ceramic sculptures, such as *The Frogman*. This anthropomorphic fauna was conceived in solitude; it seems to have crept from the undergrowth and marshes, redolent of damp life and slow decay, the very antithesis of Carriès'calm, gentle sculptures, notably his series of babies'heads.

Dampt, Charpentier and Carabin soon began to work on sets of furniture. Carabin proudly presented the *Bookcase* commissioned by the engineer Henry Montandon, in his workshop in March 1890, but he was not admitted to the Salon des Indépendants. However, in 1891 he brilliantly represented the decorative arts exhibited at the Salon of the Société Nationale des Beaux-Arts. Gustave Geffroy explained the symbolism of the figures that inhabited the furniture: "The figures close to the ground are the lowly passions, the enemies of intelligence, conquered and enslaved by the book. On one side there is Ignorance... On the other, the superimposed masks of Vanity, Avarice, Intemperance, Anger, Folly, Hypocrisy... At the top, the bookcase takes on its full intellectual significance in three emblematic figures... Truth in the centre... Reading to the right and left..."

The *Fountain and Washstand* found a buyer as soon as it was exhibited at the Salon of the Société Nationale des Beaux-Arts in 1898. It is a powerful, sensual composition showing a naked nymph astride a goatskin that she is squeezing to make water squirt into a pewter dish shaped like a pond, with two superb water lilies on the rim to serve as soap holders. The glazed stoneware, which varies in colour and texture for the bare, tender flesh of the nymph or the rough leather goatskin, adds to the sensuality and strangeness of the scene.

Dampt designed a full set of furniture for the drawing room of the Countess of Béarn (1900-1906); the style was restrained and the overall harmony controlled by the artist. The rectangular room, lit by an overhead dome, was lined with soberly decorated panels of oak, ash or elm. Dampt used the knots in the wood as part of the decoration. As in Charpentier's dining room furniture, functional elements were perfectly integrated; the bookcases were built into the walls. Above the wooden wainscoting was a stucco decoration in pale greens and yellows, with a delicate pattern of ears of wheat and olive branches.

François-Rupert Carabin
Sculptor
1862-1932
Bookcase
1890
Walnut, wrought iron
290 x 215 x 83 cm
Purchased in 1983

François-Rupert Carabin
1862-1932
Washstand
1898
Walnut, glazed stoneware,
pewter
190 x 45 cm
Gift from the Friends of
the Musée d'Orsay, 2002

The simple decoration formed of wooden panels and stucco, all with natural motifs, the mantelpiece topped with a marble low-relief designed by Dampt and showing *The Ideal Knight,* the colours and the shapes were all conducive to peaceful reflection, in accordance with the patron's wishes. Dampt designed everything in the room: the fire dogs, the shovel and fire tongs, the electric light fittings and the furniture itself, a writing table and an armchair with a curved back, a long wooden table, benches covered with gold-striped leather and the curtains.

The sculptor and medal maker Alexandre turned his hand to a variety of trades – pewter maker, embosser, lithographer, chaser, medallist, cabinetmaker – generously wanting his work to be available to a wide public. For many years he led a nomadic life, participating in secessionist salons: in Paris, with the Société nationale des Beaux-Arts, where he exhibited his work from 1890 onwards, and in Brussels, with the XX. He first earned recognition in Belgium.

About 1900, the banker Adrien Bénard, wanting to modernise his house in Champrosay, commissioned Charpentier to furnish the dining room. Incidentally, Bénard was also one of the promoters of the Paris Metro, and it was through his influence that the company called on Guimard.

Charpentier had to make do with a room divided in half by a huge beam supported by two metal columns; he designed two carved pillars giving rise to a central arch which was purely decorative but appeared to support the beam. The walls were covered with mahogany panels decorated with fine, supple climbing plants; the fittings included two side-boards, two corner cabinets for displaying silver and a large stoneware dish by Bigot. Above the panels was a series of curved columns which stood out from a frieze of ceramic tiles. Charpentier also designed all the furniture, of which only the large centre table remains; the twenty-four chairs, the chandelier and the light fittings have unfortunately disappeared.

This is one of the few complete sets of Art Nouveau furniture, in which Charpentier achieved perfect harmony, emphasised by the supple, airy shapes and the subtle alliance of materials and colours.

The painter Lévy-Dhurmer used oak and elm bur to decorate the Paris residence of the manufacturer Auguste Rateau. He worked on the project firstly in 1908-1910, then after the First World War, producing one of the very last Art Nouveau decors in Paris. This large drawing room couch illustrates the style of the late Art Nouveau movement: it is lower, more open in design, with straight lines curving in slightly at the corners, while the decorative plant forms are highly stylised and concentrated on a few parts of the furniture.

Alexandre Charpentier
Sculptor
1856-1909
Alexandre Bigot
Ceramist
1862-1927
H.E. and L. Fontaine
Foundry, Paris
Dining Room Woodwork

Commissioned by Adrien
Bénard for his house at
Champrosay
1900-1901
Mahogany, oak and
poplar, gilt-bronze, glazed
stoneware
346 x 1,055 x 621 cm
Purchased in 1977

Thonet Brothers
Firm founded in 1853, in
Vienna
Model N°. 4
Bent beechwood,
canework
H. 90 cm
Purchased in 1984

Adolf Loos
1870-1933
J. & J. Kohn
*Model designed for Cafe
Museum*
Circa 1898
Bent beechwood,
canework
87 x 42.5 x 51 cm
Purchased in 1981

Made known through exhibitions organized by avant-garde groups (Libre Esthétique, Secession, etc.), and through abundantly illustrated decorative art journals and anthologies, in the early 1890s art nouveau spread to every major city in Europe: Barcelona, Milan, Prague, Darmstadt, Vienna, Glasgow... Paris attracted the Czech Alphonse Mucha, who decorated the Fouquet jewellery boutique and published *Documents Décoratifs,* the Italian Carlo Bugatti, known for his pieces of furniture covered in parchment, the Englishman Louis Welden Hawkins, etc. Partisans of "Art in all" these artist attempted to impose their ideals of a modern aesthetic, which they thought should be accessible to everyone.

In the 1850s in Vienna, Michael Thonet launched the manufacturing of light bentwood furniture, developing a whole range of café, hotel, and restaurant furniture that was inexpensive, durable, comfortable, and whose simple forms contrasted the historicizing styles of the time, and responded to the demand for mass production.

Starting 1869, Thonet's competition, the firm J. & J. Kohn, exploited the same process and sought to extend this production to furniture for the home. J. & J. Kohn called on the services of the architect Gustav Siegel, a student of Josef Hoffmann, to design the company's booth at the 1900 World's Fair in Paris. Seduced by the formal quality and technique of a manufacturing process capable of reconciling high-quality craftsmanship with the constraints of industrial production, Adolf Loos entrusted the Kohn firm with the production of his chairs designed for the Cafe Museum in Vienna (1898-1899), whose elegance and lightness recall Michael Thonet's first designs. Kohn also produced the bent beechwood and perforated plywood chairs that Josef Hoffmann had designed for the Purkersdorf Sanatorium (1904-1906) as well as his famous Sitzmaschine Chair with Adjustable Back.

Thonet frères
Firm founded in 1853, in
Vienna
Circa 1888
Model N°. 51
Bent beechwood,
canework
H. 90 cm
Gift from Mr Georges
Candilis, 1984

Josef Hoffmann
1870-1956
J. & J. Kohn
Purkersdorf Chair, 1904
Varnished beechwood,
perforated plywood,
imitation leather
H. 99 cm
Purchased in 1983

Josef Urban
1872-1933
Thonet Brothers
Firm founded in 1853, in
Vienna
Chair
circa 1902
Black-varnished beechwood,
dyed leather, brass
98.5 x 40 x 53 cm
Gift from Mrs Inge
Asenbaum, 1988

Otto Wagner
1841-1918
J. & J. Kohn
Die Zeit Armchair
1902
Varnished beechwood,
brass, canework
47 x 42 x 42 cm
Purchased in 1986

The Viennese Sezession:
Otto Wagner, Koloman Moser, Josef Hoffmann, and Adolf Loos

Imperial advisor and professor at the Academy of Fine Arts in Vienna, Otto Wagner published, in 1895, his theories on *Modern Architecture,* expressing his desire to free himself of styles from the past and to promote a modern urbanism adapted to the needs of a city undergoing rapid population and economic growth. Vienna owes the equipping of its Danube Canal and its elevated metropolitan railway to him. In 1898, he rallied together the Sezession group created by his students and followers Josef Maria Olbrich, Josef Hoffmann, Koloman Moser, and the painter Gustav Klimt the year before, to protest against dominant academic historicism. Economy of means and simplicity of forms were the two central assertions, as can be seen in the furniture created in 1902 for the Die Zeit news dispatch bureau: a large cabinet and desks, which formed a remarkable compartmentalized set, made of grids of black wooden slats arranged horizontally or vertically. Moser provided the cartoon for the stained glass window of the portico of the St Leopold's Church of the Steinhof sanatorium, which Wagner constructed from 1904 to 1907, near Vienna; Moser chose the theme of *Paradise* for the portico, *The Misericord Works* for the lateral windows of the choir, and also drew some of the motifs of the central cupola. The immense windows contribute to the extraordinary luminosity of the harmonious white and gold nave. The majestic and monumental forms, the hieratic face of God, the tranquillity and reverential silence of the angels, the stylized motifs – all this works together to create a simultaneously solemn and austere effect.

Otto Wagner
1841-1918
Cabinet
Model designed in 1902
for the offices of the Die
Zeit news dispatch
bureau, Vienna
Black-varnished
beechwood, aluminium
207 x 234 x 32 cm
Purchased in 1994

Koloman Moser
1868-1918
Paradise, cartoon
for the stained-glass
window at the portico of
St Leopold's Church am
Steinhof, Vienna

1904
Tempera on paper
415 x 774 cm
(total dimensions of the
cartoon)
Purchased in 1980

Hoffmann and Moser began to think about forming an association of artistic trades before 1900, based on the model of British craftsmen's guilds; and the Wiener Werkstätte was finally founded in 1903, with the financial help of the industrialist and patron of the arts Fritz Waerndorfer. In a manifesto published in 1905, they stated their agenda and listed the group's activities within the gold-smith, brass work, jewellery, leather, and cabinetmaking workshops – all likely to satisfy the complete furnishing of a house. Their ambition was to coalesce a place between the designer, the artisan, and the clientele, and through teaching, to train highly qualified designers and artisans. Their aim, therefore, was to create a luxury craft trade, in order to fight against the mediocrity of mechanically produced objects; however, their quality and the time spent on them necessarily made them expensive objects. Produced in pierced or beaten metal that was silver-plated or lacquered white or silver, they integrate into interiors by reflecting their architectural organization in their form and geometry. The Wiener Werkstätte artists employed the traditional technique of planishing for objects in metal, silver, or brass, polished or patinated.

For Margarethe Hellmann, sister-in-law of the patron Waerndorfer, Moser created a drawing room furnishing that gave primacy to empty space; subtly and elegantly exploiting slightly curved lines, it illustrated the evolution of Viennese furniture design toward simplicity and geometric conciseness (*Chair*, 1904). He

Josef Hoffmann
1870-1956
Produced by Wiener Werkstätte
Jardinière
1904-1905
Silvered metal
39.2 x 12.2 x 11 cm
Purchased in 1986

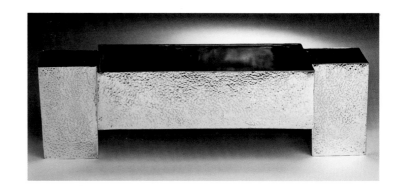

Koloman Moser
1868-1918
Produced by the Wiener
Werkstätte
Inkstand and tray
1903-1904
Silver, glass
Tray: 7 x 22.7 x 15.4 cm
Purchased in 1986

Koloman Moser
1868-1918
Produced by the Wiener
Werkstätte
Casket
1904-1905

Silk, silvered metal, agate,
wood
6.5 x 43.5 x 34 cm
Purchased in 1989

Josef Hoffmann
1870-1956
Produced by Wiener
Werkstätte
Rotating Bookcase-
Cabinet
1904
From the study of
Margaret Stonborough-
Wittgenstein, Berlin
White-leaded and black-
varnished oak, white
metal
80 x 50 cm
Purchased in 1997

designed a monumental *Music Cabinet* (circa 1904) in ample proportions. Framed by a projecting edge, it owes its refined beauty to the finish of the oak surface treated with white lead to bring out the grain, as well as its repoussé silver-plated plaques. Fine gold and silver curves undulate through the massive form like musical vibrations. This subtle choice of materials can be found again in his *Casket* (circa 1904-1905), which combines silk, silver, and agate in a work of great delicacy that is infused with Japanese spirit.

Hoffmann was then working in perfect harmony with Moser, as can be seen in the *rotating bookcase-cabinet* that he devised in 1904 for the daughter of one of the great patrons of the Viennese Sezession, Margaret Stonborough-Wittgenstein. Despite an apparent simplicity, it demonstrates originality and flawless refinement: each side presents a different arrangement and the artist shows a rare subtlety in his use of oak treated with white lead, then black varnished, in the manner of old Japanese techniques.

Incapable of attracting a wide clientele that was still drawn to the more obvious symbols of wealth in pastiches of styles from the past, this rigorous aesthetic could only appeal to a world of well-informed amateurs seeking modernity.

From 1898 on, the Secessionists Hoffmann, Moser, and their students supplied manufacturers with models for industrial production; the ceramics manufacturer Josef Böck produced porcelain dinner services by Jutta Sika, while the glass factory Bakalowits made sets of glasses designed by Moser. Likewise, while working on the Post Office Savings Bank from 1904 to 1906, Wagner asked the firms, Thonet Brothers and Jacob and Josef Kohn, to manufacture the furniture that he was designing. This included the stools by the counters and the shelf units in the managerial offices, in bent beechwood, pierced plywood, and aluminium, which are among the most outstanding furniture prototypes of the twentieth century.

Everyone had the same desire to create utilitarian objects with simple, modern forms. More than the refined and expensive productions of the Wiener Werkstätte, these mass-produced objects reached a wider public and contributed to making new ideas known.

A staunch partisan of modernity and functionalism and fervent admirer of the United States, the architect Adolf Loos remained separate from the Secessionists, whom he criticized for their lack of rigor. An individualist, he was opposed to the notion of a total art; each house must have its own style, which is also that of its occupants. The architect must help, advise, propose, and compose simple, genuine furnishings. For the apartment of Gustav Turnovsky in Vienna, moreover, Loos chose a copper bedstead and traditional chairs covered with Biedermeier fabric, on account of their practicality. In the lady's bedroom, the arrangement of woodwork and furnishings responded to the needs of everyday life; one side was for sleep and grooming, the other, for work or rest. The central bevelled glass partition, together with the mirrored screen, contributes to this fragmentation of the space, which was amplified by a play of transparency and reflection. Loos knew exactly how to create the ambiance sought after through his use of materials: blond maple-wood, brass, marble, and blue-grey silk.

Koloman Moser
1868-1918
Produced by Wiener
Werkstätte starting 1903
Music Cabinet
Circa 1904

White-leaded and black-
varnished oak, carved and
gilt wood, silvered
repoussé, white metal,
glass
199.5 x 200.5 x 65.5 cm
Purchased in 1988

Adolf Loos
Architect
1870-1933
Friedrich Otto Schmidt
Cabinetmaker, Vienna
Bedroom
Model created for the
Turnovsky apartment,

furnished by Loos in
1901-1902, Vienna
Maple wood, brass,
modern covering
Purchased in 1983

**Charles Rennie
Mackintosh**
1868-1928
Chair
Model designed in 1897
for Catherine Cranston's
tea room on Argyle Street,
Glasgow
Stained and varnished
oak, straw and horsehair
seat
136 x 50 x 46 cm
Purchased in 1979

Grouping together Margaret and Frances MacDonald and Herbert MacNairn around Charles Rennie Mackintosh, the Glasgow School of Art was born out of the context of the technological and social transformations that came with late-nineteenth-century industrial development. Their work, which branched out to include the most diverse of fields – architecture, interior design, furniture, objects, textiles, binding, posters – was shown in Paris in 1895 at Samuel Bing's gallery, at the Sezession in Munich in 1899, in Vienna in 1900, and in Turin in 1902. All of these venues were forums for exchange and meeting places propitious to the spread of a new aesthetic that sought to privilege function over ornamentation.

Rationalist and attached to local tradition, Mackintosh locked the symbolist theme of art nouveau into a rigid frame of verticals and horizontals. He decorated apartments and houses, but he mainly made a name for himself through the fittings he designed for public spaces, offices, schools (construction of the Glasgow School of Art in 1898-1899), churches, tea rooms (on Argyle Street in 1897, Ingram Street in 1900, etc.). For the Argyle Street tea room, he designed a chair with a high back topped by a pierced oval.

When Kate Cranston, a principle patron for whom he decorated four tearooms, asked him to remodel her home, the *Hous'hill* in Nitshill, nearby Glasgow (circa 1904), Mackintosh had already abandoned symbolist ornamentation and had adopted a more austere style, tending toward abstraction. The white-painted furniture, in the double guest room, exudes a rigorous simplicity; decoration is reduced to an interplay of pierced squares and rectangles, inlaid with pastel-coloured glass or with mother-of-pearl (on the drawer handles). Naturalist motifs were employed only for the mural decor, textiles, and lighting fixtures, which are no longer in existence.

The close relationship formed between Mackintosh and Hoffmann, and Loos's discovery of the United States, gave birth to a three-way axis between Glasgow, Vienna, and Chicago that favoured a return to straight forms and clean lines.

Charles Rennie Mackintosh
1868-1928
Alex Martin
Cabinetmaker-tapestry-maker, Glasgow
Bathroom Cabinet
1904

Model from Hous'Hill, Glasgow
White lacquered wood, mother-of-pearl and ebony, coloured and clear glass, lead, silver-plated brass

121.9 x 72.3 x 41.9 cm
Gift of M. Michel-David-Weill through the Fondation Lutèce, 1985

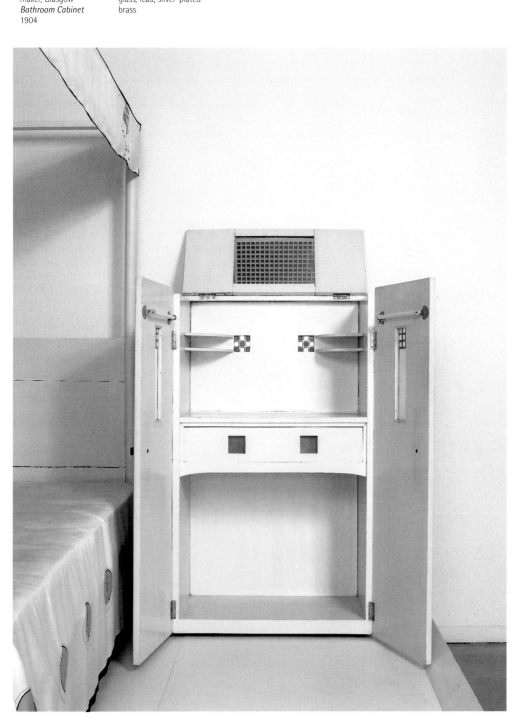

The United States:
Louis Henry Sullivan, Frank Lloyd Wright

Louis Henry Sullivan is the spiritual father of twentieth-century American architecture. He was the mentor of Frank Lloyd Wright, with whom he collaborated. The decor of the Chicago Stock Exchange Trading Room (1894) is the most accomplished example of interior decoration of the first Chicago school; there, Sullivan expressed his concept of an organic ornamentation that acts as an integral part of the structure.

In the early 1900s, Frank Lloyd Wright developed in Chicago his famous series of Prairie Houses, in which the traditional plan is broken up: wings and storeys freely develop perpendicularly around a basic core. These houses also show a desire to expose his use of natural wood, brick, or stone, in search of harmony between the house, the site, and nature. This aesthetic owes much to Wright's discovery of Japanese wood architecture with its low, horizontal lines and pure sense of ornamentation.

In Wright's interiors, seating plays an essential role in the division of space. This can be seen in the seats designed for the Isabel Roberts House (1908), which belong to a series of chairs whose barred backs act as screens, like the sliding partitions in traditional Japanese interiors.

The set of stained glass windows acquired by the museum brings to light an evolution toward a pared down, abstract style. The stained glass designed for the Darwin D. Martin House, built between 1903 and 1905, in Buffalo, employed a motif inspired by nature: the tree of life depicted with autumn tones. A few years later, the stained glass of the Avery Coonley House (1908) featured a simple interplay of horizontal lines punctuated with spots of colour, thus making Wright one of the pioneers of pure abstraction, before he had the chance to discover the works of the European avant-garde.

Louis Henry Sullivan
1856-1924
One side of an octagonal capital
1894
Fragment from one of the four monumental capitals from the Chicago Stock Exchange trading room, La Salle Street, built by Adler and Sullivan in 1893-1894, demolished in 1972
Moulded and gilt plaster
86.4 x 81.3 x 15.2 cm
Purchased in 1985

Frank Lloyd Wright
1867-1959
Chair
1908
Designed for the Isabel
Roberts House, River
Forest, Illinois
Oak, leather
125 x 45 x 51 cm
Purchased in 1982

Frank Lloyd Wright
1867-1959
Lindon Glass Company,
Chicago
Stained-Glass Windows
1907-1908
Coloured and clear glass,
zinc joined with pewter
Purchased in 1986

FONTES

MOTIF des BAS
DES
MÂT

DÔME des Bx ARTS.

DÉPART
DE
L'ESCALIER

COLONNE
DE LA
Gie RAPP.

COLONNETTE
DES
VESTIBULES.

ENSEMBLE
ET
DÉTAILS.

CHAPITEAU des PILIERS des Gds DÔMES.

Architecture

Architecture

The Musée d'Orsay has allocated several permanent exhibition areas to architecture. The building itself, being an emanation of nineteenth-century aesthetics and techniques, is an excellent example of the type of construction demanded by modern living conditions, while illustrating the variety of building materials used and industry's contribution to the new building programmes.

It was not feasible to show the huge transformations wrought by Napoleon III and Baron Haussmann, the prefect of Paris, which shaped the face of the modern capital. Instead, the museum has focused on the new Opera House, one of the emblematic edifices of the Second Empire, although it was completed under the Third Republic.

The Opera House was one of Paris' most ambitious projects, because it took fifteen years to build, involved an entire generation of artists and had a lasting influence on European architecture. The existing opera house in rue Le Peletier was cramped and had always been regarded as temporary accommodation, but none of the projects to replace it had found favour. The competition launched in December 1860 was won by an obscure young architect, Charles Garnier. The

*Maquette of the
longitudinal section of
the Opéra, made by the
Atelier in Rome, directed
by Richard Peduzzi.*
Plaster

*Maquette of the bird's
eye view of the Opéra
district, made by Remi
Munier, assisted by Eric
de Leusse.*
Wood, plaster, resin

foundation stone was laid in 1862 and by 1867 the facades were finished, but work was interrupted by the 1870 Franco-Prussian war and the new Opera House was finally inaugurated on 5 January 1875.

Located at the far end of the museum's broad centre aisle, the Opera gallery designed by Richard Peduzzi attempts to cover all the facets of the monument, its insertion in the urban fabric, its architecture and its decoration, by means of a longitudinal cross-section in polychrome plaster, showing the building as it was at the time of its inauguration on 5 January 1875, and a 1/100 model of the neighbourhood in 1914. The model makes it easier to understand the problems facing Garnier, especially the difficulty of fitting the new Opera House into the web of buildings designed by Haussmann. How could he compete with the high buildings that hemmed it in? He had to make do with tightly packed, uniform, grey facades, and straight avenues, while he dreamed of gardens, porticoes, low buildings and narrow, winding streets. But Garnier, who created the archetypal monument of the Second Empire and Haussmann's Paris, although he had to come to terms with the constraints of urban planning, rejected the features that characterise the architecture of this period. He preferred curves to straight lines, exuberant ornamentation to austerity, and a picturesque style to regularity; in opposition to the sober grey of Haussmann's buildings, he used multi-coloured marble, green and pink por-

Lequesne Eugène
1815-1887
Renown Holding Back Pegasus
1866-1867
Plaster
62.8 x 44 cm

Jean-Baptiste Carpeaux
1827-1875
The Dance
Model for original relief
1867-1868
Plaster
232 x 148 cm
Purchased in 1889

Albert Ernest Carrier-Belleuse
1824-1887
Candalabra with Crown
1873
Plaster
260 x 90 cm
Donated by Mme Carrier-Belleuse, 1891

Architecture

Maquette of the Opera stage built for the 1900 Paris Universal Exhibition

phyry, gleaming bronze and a shiny copper dome. The Opera House is confined by streets on all sides – rue de Provence to the north, rue de Choiseul to the east, rue Saint Augustin to the south and rue Caumartin to the west – and the model clearly shows the complex links between the administrative centre (the new Louvre), the Opera, the big department stores, the headquarters of the great banks and Saint Lazare railway station.

The large model showing a longitudinal cross-section of the Opera House accentuates the rigorous distribution of the various departments. Garnier wanted passers-by to know immediately where they were and to be able, without being architects, "to point out the foyer, the theatre, the stage and the offices, whose shape and nature are clearly stated and no longer concealed by an all-encompassing roof." The model also emphasises the importance of the painted and carved decor, every detail of which was supervised by Garnier, and the polychrome facade. Eugène-Emmanuel Viollet-le-Duc, whose project was not selected in the 1860 contest, criticised Garnier's approach: the theatre itself was plain and simple, so that the audience would not be distracted from the music, and Garnier focused his attention on the staircase and the foyer. In this part of the building, the spectators are the actors and the architect designed a spectacular setting for them. Opera-goers arrive through a special side pavilion, cross the discreetly decorated low-ceilinged vestibule, then suddenly discover the full splendour of the grand staircase and at last enter the theatre itself.

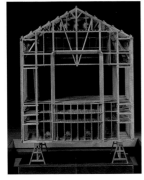

Many of the works in the Musée d'Orsay are related to the Opera House: Carpeaux's sketches for *Dance*, as well as the original stone sculpture, now replaced on the main facade by the copy executed by Paul Belmondo; models of sculptures and decorative elements lent by the Opera House's architectural department, a model of the stage made for the 1900 Universal Exhibition (on loan from the Musée de l'Opéra) and models of stage sets from the same source, exhibited on a rotating basis.

The Pavillon Amont, at the north-eastern corner of the museum, is an original display area: vertical and immense with its metal structure laid bare. Victor Navlet's huge panorama gives an aerial view of rural Paris before Haussmann's great transformations. This display explores the architectural grammar and the decorative vocabulary that the architects deployed in response to the building fever that led to the erection of over a thousand houses a year in Paris under the Second Empire, all to a strictly regulated design. At the time, decoration was the only outlet for a more personal style!

The permanent collection is complemented by temporary displays of architectural drawings from a collection that numbers some 18,000 items. Isolated drawings or entire estates (the Gustave Eiffel or Hector Guimard estates) illustrate the surveys and reconstruction or restoration work that were part of the nineteenth-century's cult of the past. They provide evidence, too, of the many public and private commissions which blossomed in a city turned into a gigantic building site, the Universal Exhibitions that strongly encouraged architectural experiments, various utopian projects and some masterly Art Nouveau creations.

Raoul Brandon
  1878-1941
  Apartment building,
  1 rue Huysmans, Paris,
  built 1911-1914.
  Ink, crayon, watercolour
  and gouache
  141.6 x 103.6 cm
  Purchased in 2002

Alfred Vaudoyer
  1846-1917
  Project for the rue des
  Nations, 1878 Universal
  Exhibition, Paris
  Pen and watercolour
  61 x 39 cm
  Purchased in 1986

Photography

Photography

Inaugurated in October 2002, the photography gallery, located on the ground floor alongside Rue de Lille, presents a rich collection of more than fifty thousand pictures through thematic exhibitions. Since the museum's conception, photography, the major invention of the century, was thought of as an essential art that should be permanently present, which is something that no museum of fine arts in France had ever envisaged. This entailed the constitution of a photographic resource, covering all tendencies that emerged between 1839, the date of the medium's emergence, and 1918, the year that aesthetically corresponds to the birth of modern photography.

Created from out of nothing in 1979, the collection was developed on account of very important acquisitions, numerous donations, and loans from various French institutions with photographs in their possession that they could not restore or exhibit. Like the other forms of artistic expression conserved by the museum, the photography collection is international. This was a completely natural inclination, since at the time of photography's invention, France kept particularly close ties to Anglo-Saxon countries, as the travels of photographers and events such as World Fairs favoured international exchange. The museum chose, of course, to bring together and show historical and original prints, made by artists from their own negatives, or by the printers of the time in the case of publications.

France and Great Britain, 1840-1880

The first photographic process devised by Louis-Jacques Daguerre, in 1837, was practiced over a period of ten years throughout the world before being supplanted in the late 1840s by the negative/positive process on paper. Nicéphore Niépce, the inventor from Chalon-sur-Saône, had been searching for a process to fix images since 1816. He collaborated with Daguerre starting 1827. A complex process on a silver-plated copper plate, a "mirror of sorts that retains traces," the daguerreotype provides a small, unique image that rarely exceeded 16 x 21 centimetres. Bought from its inventor by the French government, who bequeathed it to humanity, the process was patent-free and exploitable by anyone. Portraiture, daguerreotypists' favourite subject, sometimes resulted in superb achievements: this is the case for the portrait of *Delacroix* (1842) taken by his friend, the painter Léon Riesener, as it is for those taken by Humbert de Molard, one of the most original and most talented among the French specialists of this technique.

Starting in the late 1840s, the development of photography on paper put an end to the reign of the daguerreotype; the "French primitives" of photography began to devote themselves to prints on paper in 1840-1847. This new technique stirred the interest of the Commission des Monuments Historiques, which, in 1851, invited five photographers (Hippolyte Bayard, Édouard Baldus, Gustave Le Gray, Gustave Le Secq, and Armand Mestral) to immortalize the country's monumental heritage; it was the Heliographic Mission. Some very intimate and genuine portraits beautifully illustrate the technique; Victor Hugo and his exiled friends on the fringes of the major currents in photography constituted in three years' time one of the most original ensembles of the period, containing more than three hundred pictures, portraits of the poet, his family, his outlawed friends, exiles or visitors passing through. There, Humbert de Molard and above all Charles Nègre – of which the museum acquired a first set of images in 1981, and some remarkable prints in 2002 – stand out with their genre scenes, photographs of odd

Charles Hugo
Active since
1852 – Bordeaux, 1871
Auguste Vacquerie
1819-1897
*Victor Hugo on the Rock
of Outlaws*
1852

Salt print
Acquired under the
Acceptance in Lieu
scheme, 1986

jobs, itinerant musicians, chimney sweeps, and beggars. Alongside the commercial photography of studios such as the one run by Eugène Disdéri – of which the museum has collected more than five thousand prints – photographers like Félix Nadar, Gustave Le Gray, and amateurs like Eugène Cuvelier or Count Olympe Aguado, privileged an artistic vision. Nadar developed a model for the psychological portrait, the most moving of which were perhaps his portraits of Charles Baudelaire, anxious or nervous, in keeping with the wishes of the poet who was looking for a photographic image that had "the imprecision of a drawing." With his seascapes, Gustave Le Gray produced meticulously composed, large "enchanted tableaux" that were often attained through the combination of two different negatives, one for the water, another for the sky. The 1870s in France were a period of disenchantment; it was not until the revolution of the instantaneous photograph, in 1880, that photography gained its second wind.

The most present among foreign artists in the museum's collection are from Britain, the cradle of photography on paper since William Henry Fox Talbot, who developed in 1841 the calotype, a negative/positive process. The Scotsmen David Octavius Hill and Robert Adamson utilized contrasts of light and shadow to compose dynamic images. The museum's collection of British photography, however, mainly focuses on the work of amateurs, such as Lady Clementina Hawarden who took photographs between 1858 and 1864, most of which is conserved at the Victoria and Albert Museum in London; Julia Margaret Cameron, who was sensitive to the Pre-Raphaelite aesthetic; or Lewis Carroll, author of *Alice in Wonderland* who also evokes the world of childhood and theatre in photography, his favourite subject still being portraits of little girls, often disguised. Albums of photo-collages, mixing painted photographs with drawings, like those by Lady Maria Georgina

Gustave Le Gray
1820-1884
Marine (the Mediterranean and Mount Agde, Sète)
Circa 1856-1857
Albumen proof from two wet collodion glass negatives
32.6 x 42 cm
Acquired with the support of the Commission Nationale de la Photographie, 1990

Félix Nadar
1820-1910
Charles Baudelaire
Standing
1856-1858
Proof on salt print from
a collodion-on-glass
negative

24 x 17 cm
Acquired in 1988, with
support from the Société
des Amis du Musée
d'Orsay

Caroline Filmer or Georgina Berkeley, display the British taste for the absurd or the nonsensical. Lastly, some fine examples of documentary photography, like the reportage by Thomas Annan, *Old Closes and Streets of Glasgow*, which investigates the working class neighbourhoods of Glasgow before their renovation, complete the panorama of a rich, inventive, and original period.

Photographic Explorations

Archaeologists, artists, and tourists in search of exoticism were to find in photography on paper, a valuable tool of documentation, for the publication of books retracing discoveries made in faraway lands. In 1852, the book *Égypte, Nubie, Palestine et Syrie, dessins photographiques de Maxime du Camp,* was published, the first in France to be illustrated with photographs – one hundred and twenty-five prints from paper negatives were made by Maxime du Camp in 1849-1851, in the company of Gustave Flaubert. The book was printed by Blanquart Évrard. This assignment from the Ministry of State Education had the goal of photographing monuments and hieroglyphic inscriptions; but Du Camp's pictures are more picturesque than archaeological, contrary to those by Félix Teynard, an engineer and former student of Champollion, who published a book about the same sites, with photographs from 1853 to 1858 that exploited strongly contrasted tones and clearly showed the structure of the monuments. John B. Greene and Théodule Devéria demonstrated a more strictly scientific approach and concentrated on Egyptian excavations. The most remarkable undertaking is the one led – at the request of the Ministry of State Education – by the Alsacian Auguste Salzmann, in Palestine starting 1854. Within six months, he brought back some two hundred calotypes of archaeological views showing the monuments of Jerusalem and taken with documentary rigor, sobriety, and close attention to detail.

Following in the footsteps of the crusaders, Louis de Clercq and Henry Sauvaire roamed Lebanon, Syria, and Morocco from 1855 to 1870, alternating portraits, genre scenes, landscapes, and views of contemporary neighbourhoods. Gustave de Beaucorps visited Morocco and Spain, while Désiré Charray did a reportage on Madagascar in 1863, with a more strictly ethnographical vision.

Like the American Civil War, the Crimean War in Russia shows the same images of empty, devastated landscapes, photographed after the combats. In the United States, over the course of the conquest, a taste also emerged for the new landscapes of the Wild West and its natural marvels. A commission from the American government allowed Carleton Watkins to discover the spectacular landscapes of Yosemite Valley, which he conveyed by means of large format pictures; William Henry Jackson did the same at Yellowstone and the Rockies.

Instantaneous Photography

The first cameras appeared on the market between 1880 and 1890 and it was then that many artists, painters, and writers discovered the medium; a lesser-known artist like Gabriel Loppé used the instantaneous technique to photograph Paris by night. Charles François Jeandel staged scenes with women tied up and covered in shrouds and veils ... Photography was also employed as studies for painted compositions, however, one of the greatest painters, Edgar Degas, was interested in photography for its ability to convey chiaroscuro and the opposition between black and white.

Félix Teynard
1817-1892
Abu Simbel, Large Speos:
frontal view of the
colossal statues
1851
Salt proof from paper
negative, pl. 156 of the
book Égypte, Nubie, sites
et monuments, 1858
24 x 31 cm
Allocation from the
Musée du Louvre, 1986

Félix Teynard phot.   Publié par Goupil et Cⁱᵉ éditeurs. Paris, Londres, Berlin, New-York.

Photography

In 1886, the American industrialist George Eastman devised the Kodak camera and patented it in 1889; the fact that it was easy to use allowed for the daring compositions of artists such as Bonnard or Vuillard, whose eyes had been trained by Japanese printmaking or the framing of Degas's paintings. Vuillard did some one hundred photographs since 1897; all of Bonnard's photographs were given to the Musée d'Orsay, subject to usufruct. From 1898 to 1912, he photographed his wife and muse, Marthe, his family and friends, and he preserved images from his travels.

Pictorialism

With a desire to practice photography as a fine art, British artists were at the source of the last great photographic movement of the nineteenth century. In the footsteps of Jean-François Millet, Peter Henry Emerson chose to depict peasant life, with gravity instilling a sense of eternity. It was in France that the first photography association was founded, at the instigation of Robert Demachy. It was called the Photo-Club de Paris, and Constant Puyo was also a member. Pictorialism emerged in Russia and Czechoslovakia as well; marked by Symbolism, the landscapes of Frantisek Drtikol show a mysterious Bohemia silent in the night . . . In Austria, Heinrich Kühn modernized his compositions after meeting Alfred Stieglitz, the son of a rich German-born American industrialist. Steiglitz formed the New York group Photo-Secession and developed a passion for New York as a subject matter, which he rendered through lyrical and delicate views, in the manner of Whistler (*Spring Showers,* 1903), or as a city in all-out expansion (*The City of Ambition,* 1910). The photogravures from his famous journal *Camera Work,* created in 1903, are part of the museum's collection.

Clarence White demonstrates a very intimate and feminine sensibility inspired by the pre-Raphaelite spirit (*The Kiss,* 1904). Edward Steichen, an important member of the group, was also a magnificent photographer who showed a brilliant sense of composition, and a symbolist, more painterly spirit (*In Memoriam,* 1904). Baron Adolphe de Meyer knew Stieglitz and showed in his New York gallery; the fine album of calotypes of Nijinski in the ballet *Afternoon of a Faun* demonstrates his innate sense of light. The second generation of pictorialists, which emerged in 1880, is represented by the works of Georges H. Seeley, Paul Burty Haviland, and Alvin Langdon-Coburn.

Composing his photographs like paintings, the amateur-photographer Félix Thiollier focused on the representation of work. With a melancholic poetry, he depicted landscapes of factories and slag heaps cloaked by haze and smoke. At the turn of the century, the outstanding photographs of Eugène Atget, who is often considered as the true founder of modern photography, captured the setting and atmosphere of Parisian life.

Clarence Hudson White
1871-1925
Alfred Stieglitz
1864-1946
Torso
1903
22 x 16 cm

Photogravure, Camera
Work, pl. IV
Gift of Mrs Minda
de Gunzburg through
the Société des Amis du
Musée d'Orsay, 1981

INDEX

INDEX

SCULPTURE

THE DECORATIVE ARTS

PHOTOGRAPHY

Caroline Mathieu thanks Serge Lemoine,
like all the team of musée d'Orsay, and
more particularly Françoise Heilbrun, Anne
Pingeot, Anne Roquebert, like Antoinette
Le Normand-Romain, Monique Nonne,
and, for her efficiency and her patience,
Françoise Fur.

Photographic Credits